Business Models for Industry 4.0

Utilizing Industry 4.0 technologies is essential to meet consumer expectations of personalized products and services but not without obstacles and challenges. This book provides comprehensive knowledge on the operating conditions and challenges of small- and medium-sized enterprises operating in the era of Industry 4.0 and proposes a Business Model 4.0 concept.

The authors provide insights on the general conditions for the development of Economy 4.0 and Society 5.0, the expectations of modern consumers in product personalization, customization, servitization and the SME sector's requirements. In addition, the book offers a business model of cooperation between enterprises and the concept of rapid network prototyping methodology for the implementation of personalized products. It proposes the creation of e-business platforms that will allow for better integration of the customer with the manufacturer and the possibility of greater involvement in product configurations.

The empirical research offered in this book will provide valuable insights for scholars and upper-level students across business disciplines, including strategic management, entrepreneurship, technology and innovation management.

Sandra Grabowska is Assistant Professor at the Department of Production Engineering (Silesian University of Technology). She is the author and co-author of nearly 80 scientific publications. Her research focuses on business models, modern forms of management and Industry 4.0. She is active in managerial associations and as a consultant supporting enterprise improvement.

Sebastian Saniuk is Professor at the University of Zielona Góra (Poland). He is a member of the Committee of Production Engineering of the Polish Academy of Sciences since 2015. His research interests include issues related to production management, industrial engineering and logistics, sustainable development, corporate social responsibility, particularly planning and control of production flow and modeling of production networks of small and medium enterprises, rapid prototyping and CSR in SMEs. The results of his research have been presented in over 270 national and international scientific publications including journals, monographs and conference proceedings of national and international conferences indexed in Web of Science and Scopus database. During his career, he has conducted research under several grants awarded and funded by the Polish Ministry of Science and Higher Education, The National Centre for Research and Development and the European Union.

RIOT!

Routledge Studies in Innovation, Organizations and Technology

Inclusive Innovation
Robyn Klingler-Vidra, Alex Glennie and Courtney Savie Lawrence

Organizational Change, Innovation and Business Development
The Impact of Non-Technological Innovations
Edited by Magdalena Popowska and Julita E. Wasilczuk

Public Innovation and Digital Transformation
Edited by Hannele Väyrynen, Nina Helander and Harri Jalonen

Innovation and Leadership in the Public Sector
The Australian Experience
Mahmoud Moussa, Leonie Newnham, Adela McMurray and Nuttawuth Muenjohn

Advancing Big Data Analytics for Healthcare Service Delivery
Tiko Iyamu

Open Labs and Innovation Management
The Dynamics of Communities and Ecosystems
Edited by Valérie Mérindol and David W. Versailles

Technology Brands in the Digital Economy
Edited by Wioleta Kucharska and Ewa Lechman

Business Models for Industry 4.0
Concepts and Challenges in SME Organizations
Sandra Grabowska and Sebastian Saniuk

Innovation in the Digital Economy
New Approaches to Management for Industry 5.0
Edited by Agnieszka Rzepka

For more information about this series, please visit: www.routledge.com/Routledge-Studies-in-Innovation-Organizations-and-Technology/book-series/RIOT

Business Models for Industry 4.0

Concepts and Challenges in SME Organizations

Sandra Grabowska and Sebastian Saniuk

Routledge
Taylor & Francis Group
LONDON AND NEW YORK

First published 2023
by Routledge
4 Park Square, Milton Park, Abingdon, Oxon OX14 4RN

and by Routledge
605 Third Avenue, New York, NY 10158

Routledge is an imprint of the Taylor & Francis Group, an informa business

British Library Cataloguing-in-Publication Data
A catalogue record for this book is available from the British Library

ISBN: 978-1-032-32931-4 (hbk)
ISBN: 978-1-032-32932-1 (pbk)
ISBN: 978-1-003-31740-1 (ebk)

DOI: 10.4324/9781003317401

Typeset in Bembo
by Apex CoVantage, LLC

Contents

Figures

Tables

Introduction

The Fourth Industrial Revolution was sparked by the emergence of the concept of Industry 4.0, which took advantage of previous human technological achievements in automation, digitization and communication of resources and people. The development of new digital technologies has resulted in a completely new approach to the role of man not only in industry but also in the economy as a whole. The development and implementation of the concept of Industry 4.0 has become possible mainly due to the acceptance of ubiquitous digitalization, the development of the Internet, social networks and the virtualization of many areas of life. It is becoming commonplace to use cyber-physical systems composed of intelligent devices, machines and autonomous means of transportation, which communicate with each other by means of modern information and communication technologies (ICT) capable of collecting, processing and exchanging huge amounts of information or data throughout the product manufacturing process while reducing high labor costs. In addition, contemporary technologies such as Big Data and cloud computing, Internet of Things, among others allow monitoring and efficient management of production processes in real time. Digitally supported manufacturing technologies, data mining, Big Data Analytics and ICT telecommunications are now emerging, enabling machine-to-machine and machine-to-human communication in a virtual environment.

The progressive process of digitization of all areas of the economy, which is the result of the Fourth Industrial Revolution, implies the need to analyze the effects that concern changes in the economy and society. The changes are affecting all areas of human life to an unprecedented extent. Emerging smart factories, smart cities and smart homes use cyber-physical systems (CPS), which are open social engineering systems. CPS systems use increasingly refined artificial intelligence algorithms that operate on large data sets, collected and processed in real time affecting physical processes across the entire network of relationships with limited human involvement performing only supervisory functions. While large enterprises are able to adapt quickly to the technological challenges of tomorrow and take advantage of the opportunities for development in the Fourth Industrial Revolution, small- and medium-sized

DOI: 10.4324/9781003317401-1

enterprises need support for new models of operation in the environment of Industry 4.0. Today's small- and medium-sized enterprises must be ready to innovate, quickly reorganize processes and very flexibly adapt their business operations to the conditions of the dynamically changing competitive and socioeconomic environment. This includes the use of servitization strategies, narrow specialization and opening up to networked cooperation. A significant success factor is the orientation to the modern customer and the application of mass personalization. It requires the development of new business models oriented toward SME sector cooperation while using modern digital production and communication technologies.

These models should strive to balance the development of smart technology and smart businesses with the improvement of quality of life and recognized values such as sustainability. What distinguishes the Fourth Industrial Revolution is knowledge of customer needs, which is a competitive advantage for businesses. Today's consumers expect personalized products tailored to their needs and expectations, characterized by high quality and low price. Customization and the required rapid response in the market mean that the potential of different companies must be combined. Today, it is possible to create a fully integrated system of suppliers, manufacturers and customers operating in sophisticated open networks. Therefore, specialized companies will pool their resources to produce personalized products that meet customers' needs using Industry 4.0 technologies. Correctly defining the opportunities, challenges and problems brought by the Fourth Industrial Revolution guarantees that new opportunities, or new market opportunities, will be consciously exploited.

In this regard, the authors of the book attempted to develop the concept of Business Model 4.0 dedicated to the SME sector. They paid special attention to the need to create networks of cooperating enterprises within the framework of business e-platforms, whose task is to integrate enterprises and customers expecting personalized production. The creation of temporary production networks is an opportunity for the development of the SME sector, which on their own are unable to compete for the modern customer with Smart Factories.

The authors focus attention on the critical challenges for small- and medium-sized enterprises in the development of the concepts of Industry 4.0 and Economy 4.0. They propose a Business Model 4.0, dedicated primarily to companies that pool their resources and collaborate within cyber-physical networks. The book provides comprehensive knowledge of the conditions for small- and medium-sized enterprises in the era of Economy 4.0 and the reference Business Model 4.0. The proposed Business Model 4.0 and the concept of rapid network prototyping are not yet recognized in the existing literature. The results of the authors' research can inspire researchers engaged in the study of business adaptation to the conditions of the Fourth Industrial Revolution. Relevant research areas are the required competencies of engineers and managers and the paths of technological development of enterprises, methods of measuring the degree of digitization of processes and competitiveness in the era of Industry 4.0. The book is dedicated mainly to managers of small- and medium-sized enterprises, students of management and industrial engineering and economists interested in the development trends of modern industry supported by new digital technologies.

1 Contemporary socioeconomic challenges for business models

Intelligent society creating an Economy 4.0

The modern world is characterized by instability and unpredictability, as particularly highlighted by the COVID-19 pandemic and the conflict between Ukraine and Russia. This instability affects all spheres of life: technology, economy, labor, culture, values, etc. Modernity can be described as "constant change" or "liquid modernity," in which everything changes, nothing is stable or predictable and every organization and every person must be flexible and constantly adapt to new conditions. Modern technologies and the pace of commercialization of research results make the changes taking place in companies extremely dynamic (Bag & Pretorius, 2020). However, it is not the new technologies or even the pace of change that pose the greatest challenges of today's market environment. Technological advances are dramatically changing business-to-business (B2B) relations, eliminating traditional competitive struggle strategies and fostering the emergence of increasingly complex business models. Regardless of the type of business, the impact of ubiquitous digitization is evident everywhere. A technological dominance of change in production, services, education, science and administration is taking place, underpinning intelligent automation, robotization, logistics and communication. It is the material that binds together the professional, private and social lives of individuals and even entire communities. The increase in the scale of economic activity gives an increase in the efficiency of resource use, increases the competitiveness and stability of enterprises – their business models. Joint enterprise research, marketing or after-sales service is the path to achieving joint sustainable production. The idea of Industry 4.0 determines economic change leading to Economy 4.0 (Dantas et al., 2021), which encompasses a fully digital value chain from suppliers through intermediaries and brokers to the end customer (the recipient of the product/service), regardless of who such a customer is – businessman, consumer, building owner, retail store owner, employee, citizen, passenger, patient, etc. (Cellary, 2019).

Economy 4.0 is, on the one hand, Industry 4.0 with smart factories, and on the other hand, the extension of smart concepts to many sectors, such as (Helbing, 2021) smart grid, smart mobility and transportation, smart buildings,

DOI: 10.4324/9781003317401-2

smart health care, smart farming, etc. The scope of Economy 4.0 can be divided as follows:

- technologies 4.0 applied to the Smart Factory;
- technologies 4.0 used for collaboration between factories (smart or not);
- manufactured smart things deployed in smart end-user environments;
- digital services provided to users of smart environments.

The world is currently facing many technological, economic and geopolitical changes, as well as those in the way of thinking and worldview. Each change creates new opportunities but also challenges and concerns. People must see development as a way to improve the quality of life for the average person to want to support it. Most of the public does not have access to information as to what a modern industrial plant looks like, which contributes to an emerging sense of fear in the face of information about deserted factories where robots take jobs away from people. In the face of such a situation, it's easy to develop public resentment and fear of technological advances.

Economy 4.0 can be defined as a system of intertwining forces in the form of Society 4.0 and Industry 4.0 and Industry 5.0. Undoubtedly, their base is the development of digital technologies and their widespread use. A key feature of Economy 4.0 is the networking of its participants, their social and economic life, as well as the integration of data taken from the network.

Few people know that as agricultural productivity and production increases, employment in the sector falls, but unemployment also falls. This is because when a society has a material existence, natural human creativity and imagination are awakened, giving rise to an unlimited number of services (new jobs) that can be provided to one another. N. Keidanren believes that, without a doubt, creativity and imagination should be the key to shaping the future (Keidanren, 2016. Changes in the pursuit of 4.0 and even 5.0 by societies and economies are fostering opportunities and threats, as shown in Table 1.1 (Saniuk et al., 2020). Table 1.1 lists the opportunities and threats in Economy 4.0 from the customer/consumer, producer and employee perspectives.

Table 1.1 Opportunities and threats in Economy 4.0 from the perspective of the customer/consumer, producer and employee

Opportunities	*Threats*
Customer	
• Personalized satisfaction of consumption needs individualization of manufacturing processes (generation of high-quality and highly customized products) • Including individual customer-specific criteria in the process of production • Rapid transferring of customer requirements into production processes	• Increase in external demand by increasing the competitive advantage of foreign solution providers I 4.0 • Uncontrolled disclosure of preferences by the customer may threaten his anonymity • Crossing the border between sales persuasion and surveillance

(*Continued*)

Table 1.1 (Continued)

Opportunities	*Threats*
• Individual, customer-specific criteria will be included in the design, configuration, ordering, planning, manufacturing and operation phases, also incorporating last-minute changes, indeed enabling mass customization to be implemented • A sense of uniqueness from the process of purchasing a co-designed product • Enabling high level of flexibility • Higher usability of personalized products (best-suited product) • Enabling last-minute changes into the production process • The possibility of additional earnings by renting free resources, for example, cars, designer clothing • Being a socially responsible consumer	• Customization may make it difficult for the customer to make a purchase decision (because companies compete with each other in the scope of the offer, hence the selection of a specific product may be difficult) • The customer may not see his needs, which will not generate demand • The need to overcome hardware and language barriers in new communication systems and ordering products • The customer may feel cornered by receiving continuous information about products as part of marketing one to one
Producer	
• Creating new products with high added value • Dynamic and flexible configuration of various elements of business processes • Accurate responding to the needs of consumers due to product design for individual orders and shortening of production series • Creation of agile engineering and manufacturing processes • On-time verification of design decisions and quick incorporation of decisions into engineering and production processes • Easy access to real-time information and effective cooperation between different machinery and manufacturing systems • Monitoring operations in real time and improved information sharing and collaboration	• High costs of new investments and an increase in production costs (at Adidas costs increased by up to 30% compared to standard production) • Loss of existing outlets (companies do not gain by adaptation of mass customization because it reduces product differentiation in a competitive context) • Loss of control over autonomous factories and loss of control over business information in cyberspace • The need to identify products, for example, in block chain • The need to search for new cooperation opportunities in cyber networks – entering into new strategic alliances, agreements, and other forms of cooperation • The increased level of integration and data exchange will lead to an increase in the complexity of business processes
• Increase in productivity by shortening the production time of products, a decrease in equipment failure rate, limitation of product storage, etc. (improved resource productivity – the lowest amount of resources will be used to produce the highest volume of products, while minimizing emissions) • Continuous optimization of manufacturing processes and production systems, creating cost-effective measurement systems and performance management tools, automation of environmental control tools	• Difficulties in maintaining a balance between business and life, between high technology and life • Customer expectations are constantly rising (the customer's own designed product model may not be implemented due to the high level of unreality of its features in relation to the possibilities of producers) • The need to reduce employees along with full automation and robotization of production lines (additional social costs may appear on companies dismissing employees)

(*Continued*)

Table 1.1 (Continued)

Opportunities	*Threats*
• Improved responsiveness and decision-making (enabling proactive approach toward problem solving), improved performance and production quality, improved product development • Improved integration and collaboration • A decrease in labor costs with a significant reduction in employment	• A significant increase in remuneration for employees with unique competencies • A large gap in knowledge of sustainable development models in Industry 4.0
Employee	
• Possibility to improve work–life balance through remote work • The new flexibility will enable more flexible work organization models, which will gradually meet the growing need of employees to strike a better balance between their work and private lives • New opportunities to train and acquire new skills and new knowledge • New jobs with high added value focused around automation, IT and human–machine interfaces • Improvement of work safety (resignation from work in conditions harmful to employees' health, dangerous work will be done by devices/machines/robots) • Overcoming barriers to the physical accessibility of an employee simultaneously in many places through the possibility of providing work at a distance (virtual work)	• Risk of losing a job (especially in the case of performing physical work or not requiring many operations – simple operation of devices) • Risk of inadequate adjustment of employees' qualifications to new jobs due to lack of access to new forms and directions of education • Temporary employment forms for the duration of projects, intensification of employment in the systems: virtual work, teleworking, etc., which, in turn, can lead to loosening of the bonds in the employer–employee system • strong polarization of workplaces, manifesting itself in an almost complete elimination of positions requiring a medium level of competence (machine operators, maintenance)

Source: Saniuk, S., Grabowska, S., & Gajdzik, B. (2020). Social expectations and market changes in the context of developing the Industry 4.0 concept. *Sustainability*, *12*(4), 1362.

In 2016, Keidanren published a declaration on "Toward the Realization of a New Economy and Society – Reforming the Economy and Society," which established Society 5.0 as a new vision for the further responsible development of society. This author defined Society 5.0 as a human-centered society that balances economic progress with solving social problems through a system that strongly integrates cyberspace and physical space. Artificial Intelligence, Big Data, the Internet of Things – these are just some of the areas of research and development that are becoming elements of everyday life. Everyone's life is becoming saturated with digital data and information technology, through which we develop and share ideas, which in turn generate new business ideas. With the advent of smartphones, new ways of shopping, new ways of working and so on, the picture of the world and everyone's daily life is changing greatly. Digital technology is enabling the next industrial revolution, thereby changing the previous manufacturing-centered society into an intelligent society whose attribute is information (Keidanren, 2016).

Five stages of society's transformation from Society 1.0 to Society 5.0 can be distinguished. Society 1.0, known as hunter-gatherer society, focused on acquiring food by collecting edible plants and hunting. Society 2.0, called agricultural, developed through the "agricultural revolution." Society 3.0, referred to as industrial, is a type of society influenced by the "industrial revolution," through which the number of people employed on the land declined and the population employed in industrial plants grew. Society 4.0, on the other hand, is an information society, in which information becomes a commodity, treated as a special intangible good, equivalent to or more valuable than even material goods. Society 5.0, on the other hand, is human-centered; it balances economic progress with solving social problems through a system that strongly integrates cyberspace and physical space.

The Japanese government made an analysis and, based on this, developed the "Fifth Science and Technology Base Plan," which was adopted in January 2016. The plan calls for a transition from Industry 4.0 to Society 5.0, in which all aspects of society, including industrial work, are shaped by the latest techniques and technologies. Japan has faced the need to develop a new model for how society will function as it experiences problems of energy shortages and foreign imports, limited natural resources and an aging population. Policy makers' main idea is to use artificial intelligence (AI) to solve long-term social and economic problems. In doing so, the Japanese government has developed the Japan Revitalization Strategy 2015 as well as the Japan Growth Strategy 2017, outlining how it will work to promote economic growth in key areas of the economy. New economic growth will be supported by the development of AI and the relentless robotization of society and automation of industry with ubiquitous, super-fast communications.

In the information society – also called Society 4.0 – knowledge and information are insufficiently shared. Members of cross-sector teams do not adopt the same values, which limits the potential outcomes of collaboration in society (Palazzeschi et al., 2018). Society 5.0 suggests using advanced technologies and products to connect people and things and articulates the need to share all kinds of knowledge and information in creating new social and business chains (Shiroishi et al., 2018). Society 5.0 envisions the use of modern technologies and information solutions to free people from exhausting routine work and improve the use of available information (Nakanishi, 2019).

Society 5.0 is defined as a human-centered society in which economic progress, containing solutions to social issues, is balanced by a system that offers a high integration of digital and real space (Deguchi et al., 2020). Thus, we are talking about a society characterized by a higher level of integration, the interpenetration of both realities – digital and real – facilitating the embedding of cyberspace in the real world. Such a society can be also called a superintelligent society or a creative society. This is the next society, after the hunting society, agrarian society, industrial society or finally information society, that we have today (Fukuyama, 2018).

According to B. Salgues (2018), the idea of Society 5.0 is not a utopian vision of the future but a concept that shows one version of where the world – or at least the richer part of it – is heading. Society 5.0 is expected to affect all aspects of daily life but focuses mainly on nine areas, such as cities and regions, energy, disaster prevention, health care, agriculture and food, logistics

Table 1.2 Areas of economic and social change in Society 5.0

Area	*Action*
Cities and regions	• Better sharing of data on energy, transportation, water, waste, human traffic, etc. • Decentralization of communities in suburbs and rural areas; respect for diversity
Energy	• Development of affordable sustainable energy • Development of systems responsive to local conditions
Disaster prevention	• Information sharing between organizations • Use of digital technologies • Continuation of medical and disaster relief services
Health care	• Focus on prevention and individualized health care • Access to individualized life-stage data, using computerized medical platforms • Telemedicine
Agriculture and food	• Using technology to grow crops and optimize them • Incorporating various stakeholders into the food value chain
Logistics	• Using technology to automate logistics • Data sharing throughout the supply chain • Personalized products to meet specific customer needs
Manufacturing and services	• Service-oriented rather than hardware-oriented • Customers will be able to order items designed specifically for their needs • Support for small businesses to produce quality goods
Finance	• Diversification of financial services using digital technology • Better distribution of funds throughout society • Better access to financial services based on the use of cryptocurrency and the token economy, such as blockchain
Public service	• Improving government services based on digitization and better data exchange • Establishing a safety net in response to priority security areas

Source: Own study based on Keidanren, 2016.

and services, finance and health care. Key activities have been assigned for each area, as shown in Table 1.2.

Analyzing the previous considerations, one can define Society 5.0 as the concept of a modern, forward-looking and human-centered society, in which the integration of cyberspace and the real world is to be realized by means of cutting-edge technologies such as AI, the Internet of Things, robotics and Big Data. Society 5.0 aims to create a world in which essential goods and services will be delivered to anyone at anytime and anywhere, regardless of region, age, gender, language or other limitations. It aims to simultaneously achieve economic growth and prosperity and overcome social challenges, thereby contributing to the well-being of the global community.

Society 5.0 and Industry 4.0

T. Salimova et al. (2019) link the concept of Industry 4.0 with Society 5.0, which determines technological transformations with due regard to social aspects.

Human-initiated challenges beyond the limits of technological and organizational-economic transformation of industrial production are based on innovative development projects. Society 5.0, referred to as the smart society, integrates three elements driving social innovation: data, information and knowledge.

The accumulation and sharing of knowledge can be considered the primary purpose of cyberspace, where computer networks enable the sharing of information and knowledge without temporal and spatial limitations. Cyberspace can facilitate knowledge accumulation and sharing in many ways. As long as we focus on the "knowledge production" aspect, we can aptly describe Society 5.0 as a knowledge-intensive society. Conversely, if we focus on the "data production" aspect, we can call it a data-driven society. In the coming knowledge-intensive society, technology will play a key role in building an information integration architecture (Pereira et al., 2020). An architecture that makes it possible to collect, synthesize data and then integrate it with information in heterogeneous domains. At the same time, this will require the establishment of rules and standards governing how the collected data is used (Deguchi et al., 2020). Society 5.0 should strike a balance between economic progress and solving social problems through a system that largely integrates cyberspace and physical space (Polat & Erkollar, 2020).

Japan, therefore, wants to be a model of a new society in which various social challenges can be solved, realizing the vision of Industry 4.0 in every industry and area of society. In this way, the society of the future will be one in which new values and services are constantly created, making people's lives more convenient while ensuring sustainable and balanced development. The combination of Industry 4.0 with Society 5.0 is summarized in Table 1.3. The summary is presented with reference to the source of the concept's origin, subject scope, key components, impact on the business model and performance measurements.

Table 1.3 Industry 4.0 and Society 5.0

Industry 4.0	*Society 5.0*
Source	
• High-Tech Strategy 2020 (technology development strategy of the German government) • Strategic initiative Industrie 4.0 (recommendations of representatives of German business, industry and science for the implementation of the government program shaping revolutionary changes in industry)	• Japan Revitalization Strategy 2015 • Japan Growth Strategy 2017
Scope of subject	
• Smart Factory • Manufacturing-focused solutions • Mass customization • Servitization • Cyber-physical networking	• A superintelligent society

(*Continued*)

Table 1.3 (Continued)

Industry 4.0	*Society 5.0*
Key components	
• Cyber-physical space • Industrial Internet of Things • Big Data • Augmented reality • Autonomous robots • Cloud computing • Technologies for supporting cybersecurity • Virtual reality	• Highest degree of convergence of cyberspace with physical space • Sustainable economic development that takes into account solving social problems • Human-centered society
Impact on the business model	
• Ability to create new business models supported by modern technology • Using the diffusion of innovations to create competitive business models	• Need to create new customer experiences • Need to create new, surprising products/services • New forms of B2C communication and cooperation
Performance measurements	
• Creating new value • Minimizing production costs	• The degree to which economic progress is balanced with solving social problems through the provision of goods and services

Source: Own elaboration based on Deguchi et al., 2020.

Both the concepts of Industry 4.0 and Society 5.0 emphasize the use of modern technologies, including those related to the industrial Internet of Things, AI and Big Data analytics. Similarly, both concepts entail a top-down, state-led approach to cooperation between industry, academia and the government sector. However, there are some differences. Industry 4.0 focuses on building smart factories, while Society 5.0 calls for creating a superintelligent society. In addition, while both visions advocate the use of cyber-physical systems, the scope of their implementation differs. In Industry 4.0, the system is to be deployed in the manufacturing environment, while in Society 5.0, it is to be deployed throughout the community, with no separation between the personal and work life spaces. The two visions also differ in terms of performance measurement. Industry 4.0 seeks to create new value and minimize production costs, so the selection of indicators to measure outcomes is relatively straightforward. Society 5.0, on the other hand, seeks to create a super-smart society. The attributes of both concepts are shown in Figure 1.1.

According to Japan's 2017 Comprehensive Strategy for Science, Technology and Innovation,

> success would be measured by how far a society can "balance" economic progress with solving social problems by providing goods and services that specifically address a variety of latent needs, regardless of location, age and

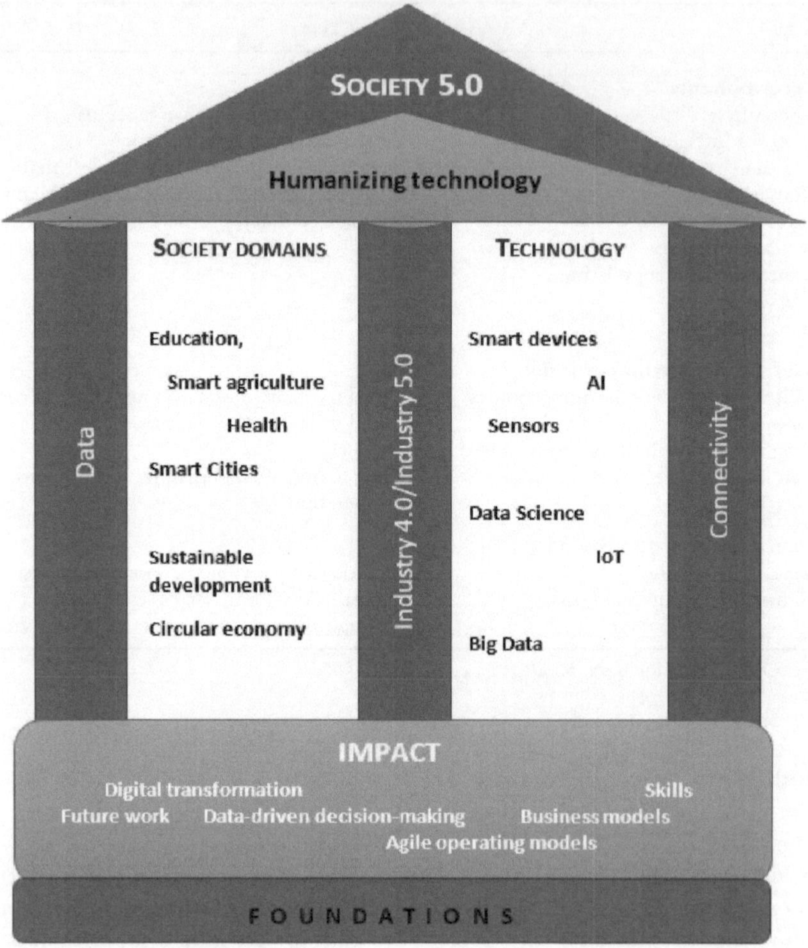

Figure 1.1 Attributes of Industry 4.0 and Society 5.0

Source: Own study.

> gender to ensure that all citizens can lead high quality lives full of comfort and vitality.
>
> (Japan Growth Strategy, 2017)

There is also a significant difference in the expected impact of technological innovation. Industry 4.0 calls for a manufacturing-focused industrial revolution but does not specify how such a revolution might affect society. In contrast, as the concept of a people-centered society implies, Society 5.0 focuses largely on the public impact of technology and the need to create a better society. Within the vision of Society 5.0 is the implementation of reform to meet the complementary needs of humanity (Potočan et al., 2021; Trehan et al., 2022).

Both Society 5.0 and Industry 4.0 reflect the responses of Japan and Germany to global initiatives and make a statement to the international community. Both concepts seek to integrate information across industries and sectors and both face the same challenges. They face the need to overcome regulatory and technical bottlenecks that are obstacles to building the necessary cyber architecture and the need to establish international standards and international information security institutions (Raharja, 2019; Berawi, 2019). This, in turn, is essential to building such an architecture. Many commentators note that Western countries are leading the way, so Japan must continue to build an information integration architecture while following global trends. Both concepts seek to build a global cyber architecture that can serve as a secure environment for creative activities. A key factor that will determine their success in achieving this goal will be cooperation with Western countries, China and the international community (Onday, 2019; Granrath, 2019).

For Society 5.0, one of the key challenges is balancing the needs of society with the needs of the individual. The actors involved in policy and technology must work together so that everyone can understand how each proposal from both parties/partners in this dialogue or technological development fits into and contributes to Society 5.0 (Carayannis & Morawska-Jancelewicz, 2022). Otherwise, these actors will pursue their own specific technologies or policies in an uncoordinated manner, without understanding how they fit into the larger picture of Society 5.0 (Huand et al., 2022).

Sustainable production versus sustainable consumption

In 2015, UN member states unanimously adopted the resolution "Transforming Our World: 2030 Agenda for Sustainable Development," containing 17 Sustainable Development Goals. Indicators have been established for each task included in the agenda, so that progress toward the goals is monitored around the world. Under the aegis of the United Nations, the efforts of governments, business and nongovernmental organizations have been integrated. Global climate, economic and social challenges have reached a scale and level of complexity that cannot be solved at the level of an individual or even a single organization and a single country (17 Goals Campaign) (Agbedahin, 2019; Weiland et al., 2021).

Sustainability is among the most important goals of developed countries. With the world's natural resources dwindling, it has become a major challenge for producers and consumers to act on the principle of "how to get more by using less." To deal with this challenge at a time of rapid climate change and increasing demand for energy and resources, a whole range of strategies and initiatives have been introduced aimed at sustainable consumption and production. These should contribute to an overall increase in the environmental performance of products throughout their life cycle, to increasing demand for better products and production technologies and to consumers making informed choices. A key role in creating a sustainable Economy 4.0 is played by Society 5.0 striving for the highest possible level of sustainable consumption and Industry 4.0 striving for the highest possible level of sustainable production. These activities are expected to lead to the reduction of harmful effects of consumption and production on the state of the environment and the protection of natural resources. Figure 1.2 shows the concept of sustainability of Economy 4.0.

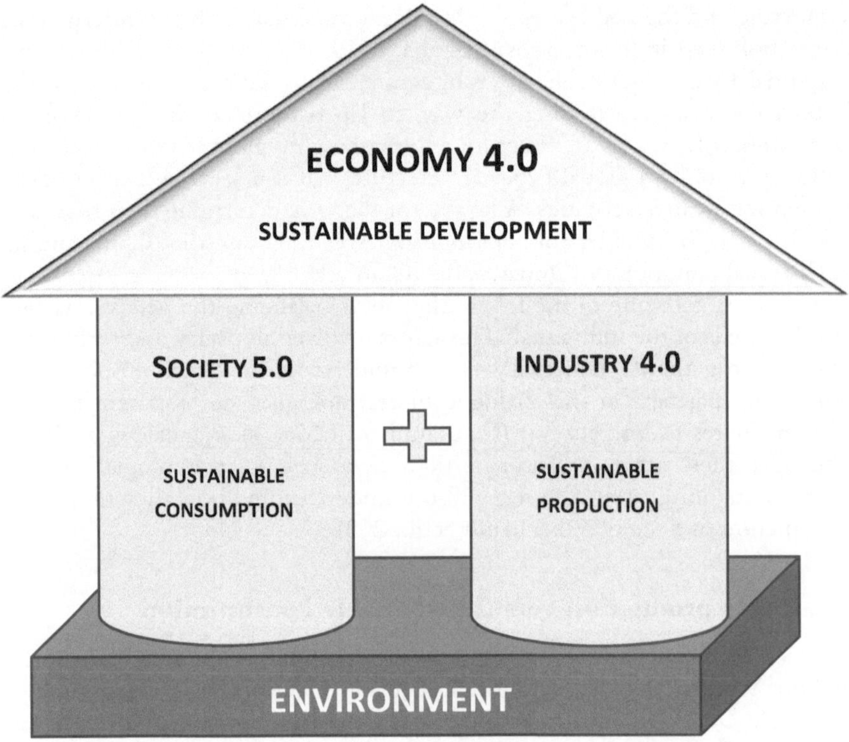

Figure 1.2 Schematic concept of sustainable development of Economy 4.0

Source: Own study.

The challenge for developing economies is to balance economic growth and the pursuit of prosperity with environmental concerns. To achieve this goal, it is necessary to balance the three aspects of development: economic, social and environmental, which necessitates continuous improvement of products and optimization of production technologies, so that with the least possible consumption of raw materials and impact on the environment, to produce products with the best possible performance and economic profitability. Table 1.4 shows the goals to lead to sustainable development. Based on the Agenda for Sustainable Development, 11 goals are presented to which reference is made to the concepts of Economy 4.0, Industry 4.0 or Society 5.0. The importance of the goals with the broadest scope is assigned to Economy 4.0, those of a social nature to Society 5.0 and those with manufacturing aspects to Industry 4.0.

Table 1.4 Goals leading to sustainable development

No.	*Goal*	*Concept reference*
12.1	Implement a ten-year framework of programs on sustainable consumption and production; all countries take action, with developed countries taking the lead – taking into account the development and capabilities of developing countries.	Economy 4.0
12.2	By 2030, achieve sustainable management and efficient use of natural resources.	Economy 4.0
12.3	By 2030, halve global per capita food losses at the retail and consumer level and reduce food losses in production and supply chains, including post-harvest losses.	Industry 4.0 Society 5.0
12.4	By 2020, achieve environmentally sound management of chemicals and all wastes throughout their life cycle, in accordance with established international frameworks and significantly reduce their release into air, water and soil to minimize their adverse effects on human health and the environment.	Industry 4.0
12.5	Significantly reduce waste generation through prevention, reduction, recycling and reuse by 2030.	Industry 4.0
12.6	Encourage companies, especially large and transnational ones, to adopt sustainable practices and integrate sustainability information into their reporting cycle.	Industry 4.0
12.7	Promote sustainable procurement practices in line with national policies and priorities.	Industry 4.0
12.8	By 2030, provide people around the world with adequate information and awareness of sustainable development and lifestyles in harmony with nature.	Society 5.0
12.a	Support developing countries to strengthen their scientific and technological capacity to transition to more sustainable consumption and production models.	Economy 4.0
12.b	Develop and implement tools to monitor the impact of sustainable development on sustainable tourism that creates jobs and promotes local culture and products.	Industry 4.0
12.c	Rationalize inefficient fossil fuel subsidies that encourage wasteful consumption by eliminating market distortions in accordance with national conditions, including by restructuring taxation and phasing out these harmful subsidies, if any, to reflect their environmental impact in full consideration of the special needs and conditions of developing countries and minimizing any adverse impact on their development in a way that protects the poor and affected communities.	Economy 4.0

Source: Own elaboration.

Nowadays, customers expect products tailored to their personal preferences, tastes, needs and lifestyles. They want to influence the configuration of manufactured products but at the same time demand a price similar to products offered in mass production (Grabowska & Saniuk, 2022). Therefore, there is a need for an entirely new, more modern and innovative approach to production and business management, which will significantly increase flexibility, efficiency and customer focus. As Korena et al. (2015) the manufacturing paradigm has been shifted in favor of customized production tailored to the needs of individual customers. The need to offer highly personalized products to customers at low prices is forcing companies to change their modus operandi today. There is a higher level of interaction between the company and the customer. Customers are involved in the creation process and even the final assembly of the product. As a result, there is a need for better interaction between the customer and the manufacturer and a reduction in production costs, which is achieved by, among other things, changing the strategy of manufacturing to order, better use of resources, developing networked forms of cooperation, delegating certain tasks to the customer (e.g., co-design, assembly). Significant improvements in production efficiency are achieved through the use of material, production and labor resources (Grabowska & Saniuk, 2022).

Saniuk et al. (2020a) presented the results of a consumer survey, which shows that the vast majority of modern consumers (69% of respondents) pay attention to whether the manufacturer is socially responsible (following the principles of sustainability and social responsibility) when making purchasing decisions. Only for 3% of respondents this aspect is not important (Figure 1.3). The results obtained testify to a high level of consumer awareness and relate to the currently promoted behavior of conscious purchase of environmentally safe products manufactured by producers with a high level of corporate social responsibility.

Sustainable consumption and production is about doing more and better with less. It is also about decoupling economic growth from environmental degradation, increasing resource efficiency and promoting sustainable lifestyles. Each of the industrial revolutions to date has brought about breakthroughs in manufacturing processes, primarily enabling increased efficient and mass production of goods and delivery of services. On the other hand, there have

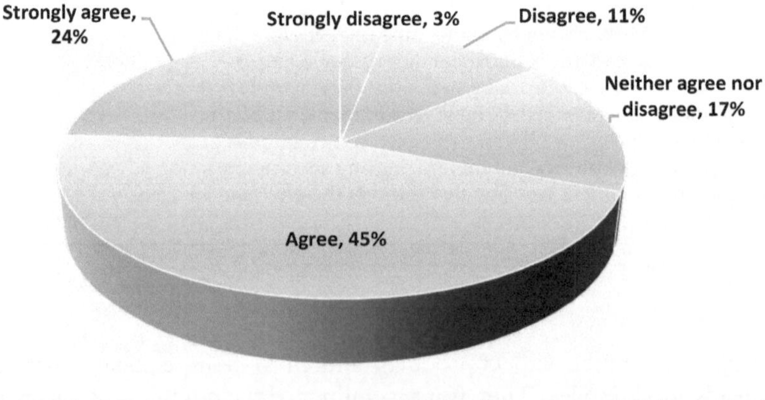

Figure 1.3 The importance of corporate social responsibility in the decision to purchase a personalized product

Source: Saniuk, S., Grabowska, S., & Gajdzik, B. (2020). Personalization of products in the Industry 4.0 concept and its impact on achieving a higher level of sustainable consumption. *Energies*, *13*(22), 1–19. https://doi.org/10.3390/en13225895

been changes in the impact on the environment, in terms of both its quality and quantity, as consumerism has led to excessive waste production. The answer to the problems caused by shrinking resources on the one hand and increasing waste on the other is to personalize production leading to sustainable consumption. This approach requires customer involvement at every stage of the product life cycle. Sustainable consumption is based on three principles (Lofthouse & Prendeville, 2017):

- Economic rationality – economic optimization in the choice of goods;
- Ecological rationality – the choice of goods that do the least harm to the environment;
- Social rationality – the choice of goods that solve social problems or do not contribute to their aggravation.

The concept of sustainable consumption is therefore an interpretation of the concept of sustainability related to consumption (Jackson, 2014). Fuchs and Boll add that a responsible consumer is one who consciously takes this paradigm into account in the consumer decision-making process. A conscious consumer is therefore an equivalent partner of business (Fuchs & Boll, 2018). Sustainable consumer behavior along the value chain is shown in Table 1.5. Consumers have a real impact on sustainability during product design, manufacturing, distribution and sales, consumption and use, as well as recycling and recovery.

Table 1.5 Sustainable consumer behavior along the value chain

Value chain link	*Consumer behavior*
Design	Co-design (such as through user-driven innovation or crowdsourcing)
Manufacturing	Prosumption (producing or co-producing goods and services)
Distribution and sales	Choosing a sustainable delivery method (online shopping)
Consumption and use	• Limiting oneself (giving up some needs or products, paying attention to technical rather than moral consumption of products) • Eliminating waste • Buying environmentally friendly products (made of natural raw materials, certified and with eco-labels) • Using reusable products • Buying virtual products (books, music, movies) • Buying remanufactured products • Buying services instead of products • Sharing • Donating (giving “second life to products”) • Lending • Repairing • Buying from manufacturers
Recycling and recovery	• Use in new applications • Upcycling and downcycling • Collection and segregation of waste

Source: Own study.

Sustainable production and sustainable consumption attempt to combine, on the one hand, the need to meet needs, improve the quality of life, and on the other hand, improve resource efficiency, increase the use of renewable energy sources, minimize waste. Integration of these elements is the main goal of modern economies, which want to provide the same or better services to meet the basic requirements of life and aspire to improve the quality of life while continuously reducing environmental damage and risks to human health. A key issue, therefore, is the extent to which the necessary improvements in environmental quality can be achieved by bringing more efficient and less polluting goods and services to market (consumption patterns) rather than by reducing the amount of goods and services consumed (consumption levels). This implies the need to change consumption patterns and reduce the volume of consumption.

The concept of Society 5.0 is radically changing the solution of social sustainability problems through a regional focus on solving and implementing solutions created from the bottom up (Keidanren, 2016; Nakanishi, 2019). This allows organizations to provide the goods that are needed at any given time, thereby optimizing the entire process of sustainable living in the local environment. Integrating technology, innovation into sustainability, enables organizations to streamline the dissemination of available sustainable solutions, create infrastructure and capacity for sustainable operation and preservation and support the development of priority sustainable areas of Society 5.0.

Despite the organization's sustainability efforts and capabilities, managers face certain limitations in adapting the mechanisms and processes through which technological development and corresponding advanced technologies occur. Technological development has so far been discussed in isolation from social issues (Savaget et al., 2019). In Economy 4.0, a broader view of technology points to the need to combine technological development with social sustainability (Rego & Polónia, 2017). Modern technological solutions support and complement the further development of social responsibility (Brunswicker & Chesbrough, 2018).

Analyzing the variety of product offerings available in today's global market, it can be concluded that consumers are getting more and more and, for various reasons, expect more and more. This raises the question of whether it is possible to create a product and offer it in such a way that buyer satisfaction is very high and remains at a very high level for a long time. The products offered on the market would not have such a short life span and would better meet consumer expectations.

Modern companies are forced to meet the high demands of consumers, who increasingly expect tailor-made products and are increasingly aware of the negative effects of excessive consumption.

Challenges of SME sector in the era of Economy 4.0 concept

The Industry 4.0 concept is the most popular in the manufacturing industry. In the most developed countries of Western Europe, over 10% of enterprises intensively implement Industry 4.0 technologies. There is a significant correlation between the size of companies and the implementation of Industry 4.0. Large companies are much more advanced in implementing Industry 4.0 technologies and using IT systems that allow for the integration and communication of their production plants or resources than small- and medium-sized enterprises. The concept of Industry 4.0 is quite difficult to implement quickly due to its high complexity and the lack of a single technological innovation. It is instead a set of related technologies that, only when implemented together, can produce beneficial results.

Another problem is the uneven development of these technologies, for example, the use of AI in decision-making processes and data analytics has broad development prospects. Different levels of technological maturity make it challenging to predict the speed with which new technological applications will enter commercial use and, therefore, when and to what extent positive network effects will be achieved. Network effects result from cross-linking outside the enterprise and increase with each additional network partner.

The wide range of technologies necessary to implement in the case of the Industry 4.0 concept and the wide range of knowledge of the skills of employees of modern enterprises is a barrier, especially in the case of small- and medium-sized enterprises. Their low preparation for the Fourth Industrial Revolution and limited possibilities of financing cost-intensive investments in new technologies should be emphasized. The lack of knowledge about the benefits of cooperation within cyber-physical networks operating in the Industry 4.0 environment is not without significance.

The SME sector is the engine of development for every economy. In all EU countries, the SME sector is the largest group of enterprises in the total number of companies. An example is a Polish economy, where, according to the data of the Central Statistical Office for 2019, as many as 97% of enterprises were microenterprises. The share of small enterprises in the structure of Polish enterprises is 2.2%, medium-sized enterprises – 0.7% and large enterprises – only 0.2%. Most entrepreneurs from the SME sector are natural persons running a business. Legal persons and organizational units without legal personality constitute 13% of small- and medium-sized enterprises (PARP, 2021).

One of the SME sector's problems is the still low use of intelligent services, such as computer-aided systems for advanced production planning and control and Big Data analytics, which are generated in the production process or through network production processes. There is no integration of existing IT systems that enable external information exchange between partners or contractors. For this purpose, it is necessary to implement cloud computing technology and related services. In the future, communication between different systems must be organized through cloud services, such as e-business platforms (platform as a service) and software (software as a service). In 2015, only 5%. All SMEs in Germany used this type of cloud service. In this respect, Finland and Denmark look slightly better, where a quarter of SMEs use higher-class IT services from the cloud (Schröder, 2016). The percentage of companies using IT systems in the software as a service system is growing from year to year. The

COVID-19 pandemic contributed to the dynamization of the digitization of processes also in the SME sector. Increasingly, small- and medium-sized enterprises use remote work, which forces them to use higher cloud computing services.

During the pandemic, the use of digital technologies played a significant role in the functioning of companies. Last year, access to the Internet via broadband was provided by 98.6% of enterprises in Poland, and over three-fourths of enterprises equipped their employees with mobile devices enabling mobile Internet access. About 24.4% of enterprises used paid cloud computing services (an increase of 6.9% yoy). Among the paid services offered in the computing cloud, the most frequently purchased were those related to the provision of email (18.3%), office software (15.7%) and storage of enterprise files (12.9%) (PARP, 2021). A similar increase in interest in digital technologies was recorded in all economies of Western Europe. As seen from the current situation of small- and medium-sized enterprises, there is no problem with access to the Internet via a broadband connection. This is a critical condition for implementing Industry 4.0 technology and using the network cooperation possibilities of enterprises in this environment.

Industry 4.0 is based on using cyber-physical systems (CPS). CPS is a combination of intelligent machines, means of transport, microcomputers and sensors capable of communicating with each other. This combination of hardware and software components is intended to manage, regulate or monitor a predefined system. The most important innovation, however, is that embedded systems equipped with an IP address and modern communication interfaces integrated with the Internet have become part of the CPS. The CPS works wirelessly and can be built into almost any facility. CPS technology can be embedded in blanks and intermediate or end products that are now "smart." They contain information about the current status of the activities performed on the product. An intermediate or embedded CPS product has information about what machine will be processed next, as long as the device can communicate wirelessly. Now, entire production processes can be virtually mapped. As a result, production can be decentralized in real time (Crowder & Carbone, 2014). These technological opportunities of Industry 4.0 pose new challenges for the SME sector. Cyber-physical networks of resources that work in the machine–machine and machine–human systems can optimize their activities autonomously and solve problems on their own or in interaction with humans. This means the possibility of networking enterprises and dividing the production process into resources located in geographically dispersed small and medium enterprises. With the implementation of CPS, the expectation of higher productivity goes hand in hand. In this case, it is possible to reduce inventory, improve personnel planning, optimize logistics and reduce complexity and maintenance costs. Product quality can be expected to increase, as well as more flexible production. Experts even predict that maximum flexibility will be achieved with a batch size of 1. This means a customized product can be made for customers at the same price as a series product. The potential savings for the various production areas are estimated to be between 10% and 70% (Bauernhansl, 2017).

These new opportunities offered by Industry 4.0 leave small- and medium-sized enterprises with no choice. To compete in the modern market, they must implement Industry 4.0 technology and connect their resources to the network. This requires modern small- and medium-sized enterprises to implement complementary information technologies. Software applications are needed to structure and evaluate the large amounts of data generated by CPS to manage, regulate or monitor customer-oriented personalized production processes. Operating in real-time rigors requires high-speed Internet and high-performance data analytics equipment. SMEs do not need to maintain the sophisticated hardware and software required to deal with sizable real-time data streams. Thanks to fast Internet connections, these companies should use the software as a service solution available through cloud computing.

A significant challenge of today's small- and medium-sized enterprises is new business models focused on network collaboration, greater customer integration and connection through trusted platform environments. Narrow specialization and the use of the strategy of servicing production systems to a greater extent are not without significance. New business models should consider close cooperation with the client during product design and production, establishing and implementing network cooperation, product liability and providing services, for example, service (maintenance) and product recycling throughout its life cycle. More attention to these issues will be devoted in the following chapters of the study.

Developing a network form of cooperation becomes a development opportunity for small- and medium-sized enterprises. Nowadays, small- and medium-sized enterprises are perceived as intelligent modules that can be used in the value network. Through business e-platforms that bring together enterprises in the cloud, companies can access missing resources or technologies required for production in real time. Also, it opens the possibility of making free production capacity available for temporary cyber-physical networks to implement personalized production orders for complex products, for example, new technological lines and so on (Saniuk, 2020). Large enterprises have the most powerful impulse to popularize Industry 4.0 because they have the required resources to switch to network production. In addition, the economic benefits obtained at the current stage of development are the motivators. The utility of Industry 4.0 increases with each new network partner. Large companies will encourage their suppliers, mainly SMEs, to gradually adapt their production techniques so that their production is more and more networked. For such development to cascade down to smaller SME suppliers, however, they will face many challenges. Large companies will achieve significantly more efficiency gains than SMEs by using Industry 4.0 technology. As the range of technology options grows, small- and medium-sized industrial enterprises will have to take advantage of the development of network manufacturing. Otherwise, their international competitiveness may be jeopardized (Schröder, 2016).

The biggest challenges small- and medium-sized enterprises face in this context are the development of an appropriate strategy, cost–benefit analysis of proper technologies and the lack of data security and uniform standards. Also noteworthy is the still low level of conviction of the SME management toward implementing Industry 4.0 technologies. For example, the study "Smart Industry Polska 2020" shows that among Polish entrepreneurs from the SME sector, there has been an increase in the implementations of the Industry 4.0 concept (in 2018, it concerned 4.5% of companies and in 2020 – 7.2%). The plans for its implementation also doubled – from 11% in 2018 to 25.5% in 2020. In addition, 30% of representatives of the SME sector believe that the implementation of digital solutions will affect the success of their company in the future. Implementing digital solutions is relatively rarely perceived as an element determining the ongoing increase in the company's competitiveness. Among these types of solutions, the most frequently mentioned were implementation of digital technological solutions – 17%, cyber-physical solutions – 13% and digitization in company management – 12%. However, the respondents expect that in the future, thanks to digitization, the efficiency of their organizations will improve. A large percentage (30% of respondents) considered the implementation of digital technology solutions as an essential factor influencing the company's success in the next three years. Other factors that will increase the capabilities of the surveyed companies in the coming years are cyber-physical solutions – 24% and digitization in company management – 31% (Smart Industry Polska, 2020). Also noteworthy are the studies conducted by the authors on a selected group of 50 small and medium industrial enterprises chosen purposefully from various parts of Poland, which already have experience with Industry 4.0 technologies and are at the stage of implementing smart factories. The survey used the CAWI (Standardized Computer Internet Interview) method. The research shows that in Poland, one of the most critical problems with implementing the Industry 4.0 concept is the lack of qualified employees (77% of respondents) in this area. Unfortunately, about 75% of the surveyed companies also point to concerns about high investment outlays in new digital technologies and too low a level of the expected return on investment in information technologies, digitization, automation and robotization of production. The low level of automation and robotization was noted by as many as 58% of respondents, as it is easy to see it is part of the third industrial revolution. In addition, it is worth mentioning the high costs of consulting in the field of technologies associated with the concept of Industry 4.0, which are a barrier, especially for smaller enterprises. This problem concerns over 55% of the surveyed enterprises. Unfortunately, entrepreneurs emphasize the continuous deficit of knowledge about the functionality and availability of Industry 4.0 technology (41% of respondents) and the lack of new business models dedicated to enterprises operating in Economy 4.0 (72% of respondents) (Saniuk et al., 2021).

The task of implementing the Industry 4.0 concept includes the restructuring of processes and the reorganization of the company at almost all levels, adjusting the qualifications of employees and strategic considerations in the development of new business models. The objections of small- and medium-sized enterprises to the transition to new Industry 4.0 technologies and the progress in the integration of various IT systems can also be attributed to the lack of standards and norms and concerns about unauthorized access to data through cloud computing technologies. The biggest obstacle to using cloud services is security issues. Of course, there is serious concern that confidential corporate information is not secure in the cloud and may be available to competitors. Further reasons for the neglect of cloud services are uncertainty about the geographic location where company data is stored and the relevant jurisdiction (Schröder, 2016).

One critical challenge to implementing the Industry 4.0 concept is access to qualified employees. It turns out executives in Polish SME companies less often admit to having competencies in digitization than in the case of competencies related to people management. They rate their digital competencies highest in data analytics and production optimization. The knowledge of these competences was confirmed by 55% of the respondents. Self-assessment of other digital competencies by Polish entrepreneurs is much worse, for example, AI (15%), digital twin and digitization of production (15%) and Big Data (22%). On the other hand, the surveyed representatives of the SME sector are convinced of their sufficient competencies in people management. They evaluate their product and production management skills slightly worse. Worryingly, over 45% of respondents do not learn about digitization (Smart Industry Polska, 2020).

Implementing and maintaining new technologies related to Industry 4.0 requires interdisciplinary knowledge and combining technical, organizational and social competencies and qualifications. In the Industry 4.0 environment, employees with multidisciplinary expertise and technical and management skills are needed. It is essential in the process of adjusting the vocational training system of employees in the industry and the process of educating students of technical universities. Nowadays, universities, courses and training do not sufficiently combine engineering with social sciences. Often, the content provided in these fields of study is tailored to lecturers' knowledge rather than the labor market's needs. Therefore, there is a need to reconstruct student education programs at universities and vocational schools.

Therefore, the modern education system faces a massive challenge of counteracting the aging of competencies and introducing continuous updating and development of knowledge and skills required by the current and future labor market (Ghislieri et al., 2018). González I. and Calderón A.J. (2018) emphasize the need to educate teachers in the field of knowledge and skills, covering areas such as advanced automation, robotics, ICT telecommunications technologies, including system integration, through the Industrial Internet of Things, Big Data and cloud computing technologies. The future-oriented educational profiles resulting from implementing the Economy 4.0 concept are, in digitization, the most sought-after specialists today, such as IT specialists, programmable logic controllers (PLC), robot programmers, software engineers, data analysts and cybersecurity specialists. Another group of specialists serving workstations, equally in demand in the modern economy, is an electronic technician, automation technician, production technician and production engineer, logistics (Benesova & Tupa, 2017).

In addition, the contemporary preparation of Engineers 4.0 requires specialized education programs for Industry 4.0, the curriculum of which should focus on data engineering, its automated collection, processing and use of data in decision-making. Examples of subjects include Data Science, Big Data Analysis, Data Communication, Advanced Modeling and Simulation of Cyber-Physical Systems, Digital-Physical Transfer Technologies (e.g., 3D Printing), Real-Time Inventory, augmented reality (AR), Logistics 4.0, Decision Support Systems and so on (Sackey & Bester, 2016).

The following problems in the studied area can be identified based on the literature on the knowledge and skills of employees involved in implementing the Industry 4.0 concept:

- New knowledge and skill paradigms are required resulting from the widespread digitization of processes, which allows to an increase the productivity of production systems and operational management efficiency at every stage of the production process (Saniuk et al., 2021; Bueth et al., 2018);
- In enterprises there is a need to employ highly qualified staff, which are open to changes, are able to transfer knowledge and work in a team (Ahrens & Spottl, 2015);
- There is a deficit in the ability to combine knowledge in the field of information and production technologies in the Industry 4.0 environment with management sciences, especially in the field of strategy development and case analysis, planning and implementation, cooperation and networks, business models, human resources, change and leadership (Graczyk-Kucharska et al., 2018; Schneider, 2018);
- It is necessary to intensify training and promote the concept of "lifelong learning" oriented to the idea of Industry 4.0 and digitization of Economy 4.0.

Summarizing the skills of employees that will be needed to implement Industry 4.0 technology, they are mainly related to the digitization of the production environment, collection and analysis of large data sets, ensuring data security and the process of effectively creating cyber-physical networks of intelligent resources of cooperating enterprises.

Bibliography

Agbedahin, A. V. (2019). Sustainable development, education for sustainable development, and the 2030 agenda for sustainable development: Emergence, efficacy, eminence, and future. *Sustainable Development*, *27*(4), 669–680.

Ahrens, D., & Spöttl, G. (2015, June). Industrie 4.0 und Herausforderungen für die Qualifizierung von Fachkräften. In *Digitalisierung industrieller Arbeit* (pp. 184–205). Nomos Verlagsgesellschaft mbH & Co. KG.

Bag, S., & Pretorius, J. H. C. (2020). Relationships between industry 4.0, sustainable manufacturing and circular economy: Proposal of a research framework. *International Journal of Organizational Analysis*, *30*(4), 864–898. https://doi.org/10.1108/IJOA-04-2020-2120

Bauernhansl, T. (2017). Die vierte industrielle Revolution – Der Weg in ein wertschaffendes Produktionsparadigma. In *Handbuch industrie 4.0 Bd. 4* (pp. 1–31). Springer Vieweg.

Benešová, A., & Tupa, J. (2017). Requirements for education and qualification of people in industry 4.0. *Procedia Manufacturing*, *11*, 2195–2202.

Berawi, M. A. (2019). Managing nature 5.0 in industrial revolution 4.0 and society 5.0 era. *International Journal of Technology*, *10*(2), 222–225.

Brunswicker, S., & Chesbrough, H. (2018). The adoption of open innovation in large firms: Practices, measures, and risks a survey of large firms examines how firms approach open innovation strategically and manage knowledge flows at the project level. *Research-Technology Management*, *61*(1), 35–45.

Büth, L., Blume, S., Posselt, G., & Herrmann, C. (2018). Training concept for and with digitalization in learning factories: An energy efficiency training case. *Procedia Manufacturing*, *23*, 171–176.

Carayannis, E. G., & Morawska-Jancelewicz, J. (2022). The futures of Europe: Society 5.0 and industry 5.0 as driving forces of future universities. *Journal of the Knowledge Economy*, 1–27.

Cellary, W. (2019, September). Non-technical challenges of industry 4.0. In *Working conference on virtual enterprises* (pp. 3–10). Springer.

Crowder, J. A., & Carbone, J. N. (2014). Cyber-physical system architectures for dynamic, real-time "need-to-know" authorization. In *Applied cyber-physical systems* (pp. 63–74). Springer. https://doi.org/10.1007/978-1-4614-7336-7_6

Dantas, T. E., De-Souza, E. D., Destro, I. R., Hammes, G., Rodriguez, C. M. T., & Soares, S. R. (2021). How the combination of circular economy and industry 4.0 can contribute towards achieving the sustainable development goals. *Sustainable Production and Consumption*, *26*, 213–227.

Deguchi, A., Hirai, C., Matsuoka, H., Nakano, T., Oshima, K., Tai, M., & Tani, S. (2020). What is society 5.0. *Society*, *5*, 1–23.

Fuchs, D., & Boll, F. (2018). Sustainable consumption. In *Global environmental politics* (pp. 83–102). Routledge.

Fukuyama, M. (2018). Society 5.0: Aiming for a new human-centered society. *Japan Spotlight*, *27*(5), 47–50.

Ghislieri, C., Molino, M., & Cortese, C. G. (2018). Work and organizational psychology looks at the fourth industrial revolution: How to support workers and organizations? *Frontiers in Psychology*, *9*, 2365.

González, I., & Calderón, A. J. (2018). Development of final projects in engineering degrees around an industry 4.0-oriented flexible manufacturing system: Preliminary outcomes and some initial considerations. *Education Sciences*, *8*(4), 214.

Grabowska, S., & Saniuk, S. (2022). Servitization and the business model of cyber-physical networks in the context of personalized production. *European Research Studies Journal*, *25*(1), 955–966. http://doi.org/10.35808/ersj/2896

Graczyk-Kucharska, M., Szafranski, M., Golinski, M., Spychala, M., & Borsekova, K. (2018). Model of competency management in the network of production enterprises in industry 4.0 – assumptions. In *Advances in manufacturing* (pp. 195–204). Springer.

Granrath, L. (2019). Large scale optimization is needed for industry 4.0 and society 5.0. In *Optimization in large scale problems* (pp. 3–6). Springer.

Helbing, D. (2021). The economy 4.0. In *Next civilization* (pp. 197–223). Springer.

Huang, S., Wang, B., Li, X., Zheng, P., Mourtzis, D., & Wang, L. (2022). Industry 5.0 and society 5.0 – comparison, complementation and co-evolution. *Journal of Manufacturing Systems*, *64*, 424–428.

Jackson, T. (2014). Sustainable consumption. In *Handbook of sustainable development*. Edward Elgar Publishing.

Japan Growth Strategy. (2017). www.mofa.go.jp/files/000272312.pdf

Japan Revitalization Strategy. (2015). www.kantei.go.jp/jp/singi/keizaisaisei/pdf/souron_gaiyouen.pdf

Keidanren, N. (2016). *Toward realization of the new economy and society. Reform of the economy and society by the deepening of "Society 5.0"*. Japan Business Federation. https://www.keidanren.or.jp/en/policy/2016/029.html?v=p

Koren, Y., Shpitalni, M., Gu, P., & Hu, S. J. (2015). Product design for mass-individualization. *Procedia Cirp*, *36*, 64–71.

Lofthouse, V. A., & Prendeville, S. (2017). Considering the user in the circular economy. In *PLATE: Product lifetimes and the environment* (pp. 213–216). IOS Press.

Nakanishi, H. (2019). *Modern society has reached its limits – "Society 5.0" will liberate us*. World Economic Forum.

Onday, O. (2019). Japan's society 5.0: Going beyond industry 4.0. *Business and Economics Journal*, *10*(2), 1–6.

Palazzeschi, L., Bucci, O., & Di Fabio, A. (2018). Re-thinking innovation in organizations in the industry 4.0 scenario: New challenges in a primary prevention perspective. *Front Psychol*, *9*, 1–30.

Pereira, A. G., Lima, T. M., & Santos, F. C. (2020). Industry 4.0 and society 5.0: Opportunities and threats. *International Journal of Recent Technology and Engineering*, *8*(5), 3305–3308.

Polat, L., & Erkollar, A. (2020, September). Industry 4.0 vs. society 5.0. In *The international symposium for production research* (pp. 333–345). Springer.

Potočan, V., Mulej, M., & Nedelko, Z. (2021). Society 5.0: Balancing of industry 4.0, economic advancement and social problems. *Kybernetes*, *50*(3), 794–811. https://doi.org/10.1108/K-12-2019-0858

Raharja, H. Y. (2019). Relevansi pancasila era industry 4.0 dan society 5.0 di pendidikan tinggi vokasi. *Journal of Digital Education, Communication, and Arts (Deca)*, *2*(1), 11–20.

Raport o stanie sektora małych i średnich przedsiębiorstw w Polsce, PARP-Warszawa. (2021). ISBN 978-83-76-33-449-3. www.parp.gov.pl/storage/publications/pdf/PARP-26_Raport-2021-07-22_WCAG.pdf

Raport Smart Industry Polska. (2020). *Ministerstwo Rozwoju Pracy i Technologii, Siemens Polska*. https://drive.google.com/file/d/19qEB4cPwsckhYfrQ1GyCF8DrrKql2BAA/view

Rego, A., & Polónia, D. (2017). Corporate sustainability: A view from the top. *Journal of Business Ethics*, *143*(1), 133–157.

Sackey, S. M., & Bester, A. (2016). Industrial engineering curriculum in industry 4.0 in a South African context. *South African Journal of Industrial Engineering*, *27*(4), 101–114.

Salgues, B. (2018). *Society 5.0: Industry of the future, technologies, methods and tools*. John Wiley & Sons.

Salimowa, T., Guskova, N., Krakovskaya, I., & Sirota, E. (2019). From industry 4.0 to society 5.0: Challenges for sustainable competitiveness of Russian industry. *IOP Conf. Series: Materials Science and Engineering*, *497*. https://doi.org/10.1088/1757-899X/497/1/012090

Saniuk, S. (2020). The platform for production capacity exchange management as a support for implementation of the industry 4.0 concept. In D. Cagáňová & N. Horňáková (Eds.), *Mobility internet of things 2018: Mobility IoT* (pp. 127–136). Springer Nature Switzerland. ISBN: 9783030309107. https://doi.org/10.1007/978-3-030-30911-4_8

Saniuk, S., Caganova, D., & Saniuk, A. (2021). Knowledge and skills of industrial employees and managerial staff for the industry 4.0 implementation. *Mobile Networks and Applications*, 1–11.

Saniuk, S., Grabowska, S., & Gajdzik, B. (2020a). Personalization of products in the industry 4.0 concept and its impact on achieving a higher level of sustainable consumption. *Energies*, *13*(22), 1–19. https://doi.org/10.3390/en13225895

Saniuk, S., Grabowska, S., & Gajdzik, B. (2020b). Social expectations and market changes in the context of developing the industry 4.0 concept. *Sustainability*, *12*(4), 1362.

Savaget, P., Geissdoerfer, M., Kharrazi, A., & Evans, S. (2019). The theoretical foundations of sociotechnical systems change for sustainability: A systematic literature review. *Journal of Cleaner Production*, *206*, 878–892.

Schneider, P. (2018). Managerial challenges of industry 4.0: An empirically backed research agenda for a nascent field. *Review of Managerial Science*, *12*(3), 803–848.

Schröder, C. (2016). *The challenges of industry 4.0 for small and medium-sized enterprises*. Friedrich-Ebert-Stiftung.

Shiroishi, Y., Uchiyama, K., & Suzuki, N. (2018). Society 5.0: For human security and well-being. *Computer*, *51*(7), 91–95.

Trehan, R., Machhan, R., Singh, P., & Sangwan, K. S. (2022). Industry 4.0 and society 5.0: Drivers and challenges. *IUP Journal of Information Technology*, *18*(1), 40–58.

Weiland, S., Hickmann, T., Lederer, M., Marquardt, J., & Schwindenhammer, S. (2021). The 2030 Agenda for sustainable development: Transformative change through the sustainable development goals? *Politics and Governance*, *9*(1), 90–95.

2 Megatrends of the Fourth Industrial Revolution determining changes in business models

Technological environment – digitalization of industrial processes

The modern business environment is under intense pressure to digitize processes due to the need to reduce costs, increase productivity and apply sustainability principles. Almost all companies are taking the direction of customer orientation and competing in the market through technological superiority, providing the customer with a better product, often personalized and produced using modern production and communication technologies. Acceptance, support and implementation of new technologies are necessary today not only to be competitive but also to survive in a very demanding market (Caputo et al., 2021; Rachinger et al., 2018).

Already today one can observe changes in the economy and society caused by dynamic technological advances. Society is increasingly using digital services like car-sharing, e-commerce, e-banking and so on, which are changing the demand for new products and services and forcing a change in the "modus operandi" of companies operating in the market. The model of producer–customer communication, the marketing used by enterprises and enterprise development strategies are changing. Personalization, servitization and network-oriented cooperation and communication of enterprises are gaining importance. Technological changes are also resulting in climatic, cultural, social changes in the forms and ways of implementing work processes, interorganizational cooperation, globalization and leading, both of individual organizations, industries, markets and entire economies (Huawei, 2021; Ebert & Duarte, 2018; Gobble, 2018).

Particularly noticeable are the changes regarding the orientation of companies to the modern customer. Increasingly demanding customers are looking for products that are better tailored to their individual needs. This is changing the paradigm of mass production, where the customer was dependent on the manufacturer and his initiative. Nowadays, the customer wants to have more influence over product selection and decide on the final shape and functionality of the product. The result is the use of mass customization strategies, which means producing personalized products at the same time at a low marginal

DOI: 10.4324/9781003317401-3

cost. As a result, there is a growing need to implement business models using, for example, co-creation and establishing close relationships with the customer (Iglesias et al., 2020) or crowdsourcing (Allon & Babich, 2020). The development of communication at the producer–customer interface has become possible due to the development of the Internet and accompanying technological solutions. Nowadays, the possibility of direct contact with customers who want to provide personal feedback on their current and future expectations for a product or service is increasingly used. Thanks to social media, there is also a systemic collection of data on individual and social behavior, which shapes the overall strategies of manufacturing companies. This changes the "producer-customer" relationship and requires new knowledge and skills from both company employees and consumers. Digitalization leads to the need for better organization of marketing activities, which must be oriented not to the sale of already finished products but to the analysis of expectations and trends identified from the huge amount of collected data from various sources.

Also noteworthy is the transformation of the value chain (Ferreira et al., 2019). M. Porter's classic value chain model is changing, becoming more efficient and dynamic. In today's model, there is an effective vertical integration, made possible by the availability of data on processes, production and others in real time. This includes all areas of the company from research and development, purchasing, production, logistics and marketing. Similarly, the effectiveness of horizontal integration is increasing. Intelligent delivery and logistics systems, as well as raw material and product flow management, are enabling increasingly efficient optimization of logistics and production processes and increasing the quality of planning. The availability of digital data and the "visibility" of production also allow for easier sharing of information between the organization and its contractors and suppliers on the one hand and customers and companies in the distribution network on the other.

Digitalization in production and logistics processes enables new e-business models. Examples include Software as a Service (SaaS), Platform as a Service (PaaS) solutions, and so on. This is particularly important for reducing high investment costs by replacing them with lower service costs. The implementation of the New Business Models approach corresponds very strongly with the concept of organizational "openness," for example, to various forms of cooperation, including networking, coopetition, strategic partnerships, co-creation and so on. This requires organizations to develop an open culture, open resources and open knowledge (Adamik, 2018).

Product traceability and the digitization of production and value chains are enabling increasingly complex enterprise and product lifecycle management. These are supported by digital design and prototyping (the creation of the so-called Digital Twin) and software that facilitates analytical, planning, decision-making, organizational or control processes. In addition to this, modern systems and methods for collecting and analyzing data on the use of products and services are helping to increasingly adapt them to future customer needs (Hastig & Sodhi, 2020; Saberi et al., 2019).

The general trends presented earlier are related to the implementation of deployed new technologies of the Industry 4.0 era. Among the most recognizable are:

- AI – which includes technologies for advanced decision-making algorithms and learning systems, systems that enable machine learning and their autonomous solution of complex decision-making problems (Zang & Lu, 2021).
- Big Data – defined as technology used to optimize processes, detect anomalies and interpret very large volumes (sets) of disparate production data using advanced analytics and AI algorithms. Within this technology, the use of real-time data analysis and production optimization (RTC) systems, which are software for processing and analyzing data in real time, is important. This allows for far-reaching production optimization and implementation of predictive maintenance methodology capabilities. This technology ensures the availability of up-to-date production execution information at the level of the company's strategic management (Haoxiang & Smys, 2021).
- Blockchain – a technology of distributed registries storing information about transactions, giving the possibility to conclude the so-called smart contracts between entities without the existence of an external guarantor or certifying institution (Javaid et al., 2021).
- Cloud computing – a distributed computing fabric technology that enables remote data storage and processing as well as resource virtualization and the ability to easily scale the system (Sadeeq et al., 2021).
- Cybersecurity – technologies that are strongly linked to security strategies, including appropriate industrial system design methodologies and the implementation of advanced security measures to minimize cyber threats, both externally and internally (Quayyum et al., 2021).
- Digital Twin – technologies and software that enable the creation of virtual representations of physical systems and their simulation (Semeraro et al., 2021).
- Incremental manufacturing/3D printing – encompassing technologies that enable low- and medium-volume production using plastics, resins and metals (and increasingly other advanced materials) while providing the ability to rapidly prototype components and produce parts with unusual shapes and functions (Sommer et al., 2021).
- Industrial Internet of Things (IIoT) – technology that enables the creation of communication systems with distributed sensors, devices and other network elements to implement technical and business solutions based on internet technologies (Pivoto et al., 2021).
- Internet of Things (IoT) – understood as a network of devices forming a spider web in which information is exchanged between them, the data that is transferred between computers is processed and stored on separate drives or external servers. They are collected without the user's consent

each time. This happens automatically, thanks to a preprogrammed action. Such solutions accompany us at every step both in private life and in public spaces. Numerous cameras and sensors constantly collect information, for example, on temperature, humidity or traffic, and transmit them to us via devices that everyone carries with them these days. Thanks to them, we can communicate with the world around us, as well as with other users. Creating such connections within a single manufacturing or service facility creates an opportunity to fully integrate the various machines, robots and equipment on the plant's equipment, making the cooperation between them more synchronized and better suited to the plant's current capacity (Nguyen et al., 2021).

- Virtual reality VR/augmented reality – technologies that enable engineers and technicians to be supported during design and maintenance work through the use of goggles or other virtual and augmented reality devices. In terms of this technology, mobile interfaces (HMIs) are commonly used, that is, solutions used in modern maintenance that provide the ability to implement augmented reality solutions based on the use of mobile devices that provide the ability to remotely access production information and control machines and systems (Emmelkamp & Meyerbröker, 2021).

The presented selected technologies make it possible to build Smart Factories, that is, plants based on cyber-physical systems, their integration using IIoT and new methods of production organization. They enable a high level of personalization of products and conduct manufacturing processes with little employee involvement. They can forecast developments so as to avoid downtime and other likely disasters in operational processes. With advanced ICT skills, they reduce the execution time of operational processes while making them more responsive. With IoT, they can communicate with production processes, maintenance schedules and the surrounding environment. An increasingly common solution to facilitate such systems is collaborative robots (Cobots) (Gualtieri et al., 2021), which represent a new generation of robots. These robots can interact with humans without the need for protective solutions, as they are machines that are safe to use (aware of human presence), easy to deploy (no specialists are needed to program them) and flexible in application. Cobots are great at replacing humans during hazardous work.

The Industry 4.0 era is generating an ever-evolving set of new guidelines. However, it is possible to identify a certain base bundle, which should constitute a kind of "core" of any smart organization (Smart Organization), especially a smart factory (Smart Factory). It is constituted by four key technologies: integrated cyber-physical systems (ICP systems), production process optimization and predictive maintenance systems, IIoT and Big Data and solutions that guarantee cybersecurity. These technologies should be encapsulated with further new so-called companion technologies tailored to the needs of a given organization. Various literature sources compile lists of varying lengths of these (Gajdzik et al., 2021).

Also worthy of special attention are the ancillary processes in industry that support the generation of the value chain of modern companies. Thus, they mostly concern (Jahani et al., 2021):

- in logistics: automation, use of robots, sensors and RFID technology, use of business intelligence software, real-time CRM software, blockchain technology for transaction processing;
- in the operation of manufacturing systems, the use of sensors, RFID technology, full process transparency, machine-to-machine (M2M) communication, robotics and networking;
- in service processes, the use of data analytics using Big Data, AI, machine learning and deep learning technologies;
- in data security, securing the organization's data, financial planning, investment and real-time controlling;
- in the field of human resource management, the use of performance-based pay, disappearing and emerging jobs;
- in technological development, the use of hardware, cloud, network, software technology development and the use of autonomous robots;
- in procurement, the use of real-time monitoring of supplier performance, continuous data flow, automation and autonomization of purchasing processes.

Business networks of cooperating enterprises of Industry 4.0

In practice, business networks of cooperating enterprises of Industry 4.0, called cyber-physical enterprise networks, are a combination of vital components of cyber-physical systems composed of intelligent resources located in individual enterprises. These components are resources (machines, equipment, logistics assets) that have communication capabilities using the appropriate data transmission infrastructure provided, for example, by the Internet (especially Internet of Things technology) and can work autonomously or cooperate with people at a distance in real time. Today, cyber-physical networks of intelligent resources cover a very wide spectrum of applications oriented to the needs of the modern customer. They find their application in all areas of Economy 4.0 relevant to the development of a smart society, including smart city systems, energy security systems, industrial production systems (Smart Factories), smart services for society, defense assurance or even environmental monitoring and protection. In each case, we are dealing with a smart organization, a key feature of which is openness to cooperation not only in the use of resources but also in the transfer of knowledge for continuous improvement. In practice, there are an increasing number of cases of such organizations that can be considered smart enterprise networks, which are dynamically undergoing process digitization and using a wide range of Industry 4.0 technologies.

An example of a Polish company for which the implementation of Industry 4.0 solutions was a strategic priority is a Polish manufacturer of gates, doors and fences (the company does not agree to publish its name). The company has invested in all links of the value chain to create a digital factory that enables mass customization of production. The brand's entire network of distributors has the tools to personalize the product for the end customer. In addition, once an order is placed, the IT system automatically generates technological parameters for production (including welding robot operating parameters and machining machine control codes). This makes it possible to realize individualized production with negligible system changeovers and thus reduce the unit cost of products. IT integration of the vertical value chain significantly reduces the delivery time of the final product, which translates into measurable business benefits. The applied robotic welding system allows to increase production efficiency several times and optimize the entire flow and order fulfillment process. The company is an excellent example of a modern approach to the customer and has the opportunity to participate in the design of personalized products and strengthen ties with the customer through the use of digital communication channels.

Another example of the digitization of processes and networking between customer and manufacturer is an internationally operating company that produces parts for the automotive sector. The company has created a platform through which production data is processed and visualized. The company is using the IIoT and processing huge data sets in the cloud. The company's data collection covers all plants, production lines, individual machines and individual products and provides insight into all performance indicators, allowing analysis and optimization of the value chain in real time. The implementation of Industry 4.0 solutions began with the definition of the company's digital development strategy in 2013. The projects implemented at the company using the pillars of Industry 4.0 cover the entire value chain but to the greatest extent – production and logistics. Investments implemented in the area of internal logistics include the use of RFID (radio frequency identification) technologies automatically registering transported items and mediating the exchange of information between production and the warehouse, also using advanced Industry 4.0 solutions, such as automation and robotization of warehouse and transport activities. External logistics includes the exchange of information in products (cars) that have already left the factory. This makes it possible to monitor products and update software at the customer's site. The modules installed in the cars have the latest available version of the software that controls them. The company stands out for the high degree of integration and automation in its production facilities. Every stage of production is handled by intelligent robots. The use of the IIoT and the company's deployment of a network of wireless sensors to monitor production and the energy consumption of machinery and process plants make it possible to optimize processes and create performance benchmarks for other units of the company. Operators are equipped with mobile control tablets and virtual reality goggles, and they have constant access to all the necessary data for constant monitoring. Factory management is centralized in one main building, which acts as a "central nervous system." Industry 4.0 solutions at the company's individual plants cover all aspects of both the production itself and its tools – materials, production, products, factory, energy management, safety technology, including the evacuation process. Even the company's canteen uses an automated meal-ordering process. The most important advantage of the solutions implemented so far is that they can be quickly transferred to other factories of the company, located around the world.

Another company operates in the metal industry serving markets around the world. In 2018, the company included in its strategy, the implementation of Industry 4.0 solutions. The development of the company's new strategy was preceded by a multidimensional analysis of data, based on internal bases. The company's new strategy is based on safety, production, management and information, as well as maintenance of machinery and equipment. The company has implemented digital solutions to centralize knowledge – knowledge is systematized, and the relationship between new technologies in the mining area and IT solutions is constantly increasing. In 2019, dedicated IT systems for production management were implemented; from now on, every decision on the optimal use of resources is based on reliable data provided in real time – IT supports the development of multidimensional analysis of data from production processes. Currently, the company is implementing about 50 projects in various areas of its business. The enterprise plans to achieve the basic level of implementation of Industry 4.0 in 2023, with its own cloud for data storage, which will also be used by contractors and customers. The company is at the beginning of its journey to build a business model based on Industry 4.0 solutions and plans to take action in many areas at once: monitoring, localization, robotics and analytics. The changes will extend not only to manufacturing but also to commerce and data processing.

The development of digital twin technology may also facilitate the building of cyber-physical enterprise networks. A digital twin is a concept that involves creating a virtual representation of enterprises, production systems or plant networks, the status of which is updated in real time. This makes it possible to monitor a given environment and the condition of equipment, as well as to run simulations in virtual reality, saving time, money and making better decisions about future products and their new features. A consortium of Microsoft, Dell, Lendlease and Ansys (a maker of simulation and spatial design software) has announced the creation of common standards and terminology for building digital twins (Digital Twin) in terms of developing rules for architecture, security and how the digital twin works with information systems, which should accelerate the development of this technology. Among the consortium's goals is to create an open source code, provide access to specialists and facilitate the building of conglomerates of companies that will tackle joint digital twin projects to lower investment costs.

Industry 4.0 solutions implemented in companies, supported by predictive simulation technologies and the use of their digital twins, bring real benefits in various areas of their operation, not only those related to production or distribution itself. The most important benefits include better utilization of resources, if only through reduced downtime, which translates into increased resource productivity. It's also cost optimization, thanks to loss monitoring. Modern solutions also mean more effective planning and management of processes not only within the company but across the entire supply chain or network of plants. It's the ability to produce personalized products in accordance with customer requirements, which translates into an increase in the attractiveness of the offer and an increase in the competitiveness of the company. It's also the ability to adapt quickly to changing market requirements, shorten the time for designing the network organization and launching new products and better control over the entire life cycle of the product (through the ability to monitor its basic parameters during use by the customer).

Customization of production and expectations of a modern customer – personalization

The widespread digitization of all areas of the economy, including modern industry implemented under the idea of Industry 4.0, has resulted in the use of cyber-physical systems composed of intelligent machines and equipment, autonomous means of transportation, capable of communicating with each other using modern ICT (information and communication technologies). Emerging systems of smart factories (Smart Factories) make use of technologies such as Internet of Things (IoT), Big Data and cloud computing, augmented reality (AR) and so on, which make it possible to monitor production processes in real time and achieve a high level of flexibility and productivity of production systems (Windelband, 2014; Ahrens & Spöttl, 2015; Pape & Rannenberg, 2019). The idea of Industry 4.0 with regard to newly designed cyber-physical production systems implies, among other things (Hermann et al., 2016):

- interoperability, understood as the ability to communicate, exchange data and coordinate the activities of cyber-physical system components;
- virtualization of processes and systems combined with real-time monitoring of physical processes;
- decentralization of resources providing a high level of flexibility and productivity through better use of the know-how of distributed resources;
- use of data analytics through real-time data collection and processing;
- service orientation and modularity, resulting in a personalized approach to the customer, and servitization.

F. Newell (1997) defines personalization as any customization of a product (its features, method of distribution and even promotion] to meet individual customer needs. Thanks to the opportunities offered by the Fourth Industrial Revolution, product personalization is now a major challenge for today's enterprises, both large smart factories and SMEs. Enterprises are required to organize production in a completely different way, with a priority on responding quickly to customer needs, in terms of developing a personalized product, delivering the order on time and ensuring a low purchase price. Product personalization differs from product customization in that, in the case of personalization, the enterprise needs access to information on customer needs, based on which it customizes the product for the market. In contrast, in the case of customization, the company does not need to have this information, as it directly engages the customer at various stages of the product development process (Szymkowiak, 2014). According to Zhou et al. (2015), in terms of personalization, its four underlying dimensions can be distinguished:

1 One-consumer market – personalization is implemented at the individual level, making the customer feel that he or she is the exclusive or preferred recipient of the service or product. This pattern can be repeated many times with each successive customer, resulting in increased customer loyalty.
2 Mass efficiency – mass-personalized products are not completely new, as in the case of craft production. In this model, the idea is to customize the product to individual preferences but with limited fulfillment costs (Kumar, 2007).
3 Customer co-creation of the product – companies in today's economy are forced to constantly adapt as a result of increasingly complex and turbulent market conditions. The involvement of the customer in the design process should not be considered in terms of cost minimization but an opportunity for higher value. Personalization in this case means active interaction with customers and the plane of product creation should be shifted from the perspective of creating only a physical product to creating new experiences and building consumer satisfaction.
4 User experience – manufacturers should go beyond the standard exploration of market potential by meeting the latent needs of consumers. Personalization requires that the product be adaptable and customizable, as not only the final product but also the basic construction, design or packaging should be able to be differentiated so that the product meets individual customer preferences.

However, within the types of personalization, three key areas of personalization can be distinguished, which are (Vesanen, 2007):

1 Product-related area – identifying product elements that customers can customize – utilizing and configuring the resources of the organization or its value chain partners to meet the diverse needs of a large number of customers.

2 The area related to the organization – the core competency in designing an efficient process is to use and configure the resources of the organization or its value chain partners to meet the diverse needs of a large number of customers.
3 Area related to customer choice – the core competency is to support customers in identifying their needs while reducing the complexity and burdensomeness of their choices.

Companies operating in today's market are beginning to understand the need for change, especially in the area of the aforementioned assumptions of the Industry 4.0 idea, the implementation of modern digital technologies and intelligent cyber-physical systems. There is also a need for a completely new, more modern and innovative approach to production and business management, which will radically increase flexibility, productivity and customer orientation. Today's customers expect products tailored to their personal preferences, tastes, needs and lifestyles. They want to influence the configuration of manufactured products but at the same time demand a price similar to products offered in mass production (Saniuk et al., 2020). According to Korena et al. (2015) the manufacturing paradigm has shifted in favor of customized production tailored to individual customers. The need to offer customers highly personalized products at low prices is forcing companies to change the way they operate and orient themselves to a higher level of company–customer interaction.

Increasingly today, customers are involved in the product development process and even the final assembly. As a result, there is a need for better interaction between the customer and the manufacturer and a reduction in production costs, which is achieved, among other things, by changing the strategy of manufacturing to order, better use of resources, developing networked forms of cooperation, delegating certain tasks to the customer (e.g., co-design, assembly). Significant improvements in production efficiency are achieved mainly through the use of material, production and labor resources. Intense competition and rising customer expectations in today's marketplace mean that as production efficiency increases, a higher level of product personalization follows (Anshari et al., 2019; Torn & Vaneker, 2019).

It can be assumed that mass personalization is a higher level of mass customization. According to M. Young, customization focuses only on overt needs initiated by customers themselves, while personalization is also based on implicit needs (Młody, 2018). On the other hand, W. Ciechomski emphasizes that customization is one of the modern forms of communication of enterprises with customers. Mass customization involves personalization of a company's offerings on a large scale, which is possible due to the dynamic development of production technologies and in-depth knowledge of consumer needs and preferences. Its goal is to optimally meet the needs of buyers by involving them in the process of designing goods (Ciechomski, 2019).

Competitive advantage in the market of modern enterprises is built through the ability to meet individual customer requirements and a high level of mass customization of production. According to A. Kaplan and M. Haenlein (2006), mass customization is a strategy that creates added value through close cooperation between the manufacturer and the customer at every stage of the production process, that is, product design, production and assembly. The main goal of customization is to produce customized products with production costs and prices similar in level to mass-produced products. In the case of mass customization, the strategy is based on providing a large variety of products so that almost every customer can find a product that meets his or her needs (Pallant et al., 2020). Today, customization requires a personalized approach to the customer, thus a high degree of flexibility and efficient organization of production planning and execution. The problem of meeting growing customer expectations mainly requires closer cooperation with the customer. J. Lampel and H. Mintzberg (1996), depending on the degree of customer involvement in the process of manufacturing a new product, distinguish four key strategies of mass customization, which are pure customization, tailored customization, standardized customization and pure standardization. The first of these, so-called pure customization, is a strategy in which the customer takes an active part in all stages of production, including the design stage of a new product. In this strategy, products are completely individualized, virtually unique. The second strategy, so-called tailor-made customization, means that the customer influences the dimensions or shapes of standard product components so that the product meets his specific needs. The third strategy, in which the customer is only involved in the assembly or distribution phase of the product is standardized customization. The product is modified and configured according to a list of standard options. The last type of customization strategy is pure standardization, where the customer has no influence on the product (Mintzberg et al., 2003; Lampel & Mintzberg, 1996).

The highest degree of customer interference, while at the same time the most expensive and difficult to organize, exists in pure customization. Important goals accompanying customization are significant productivity improvements and manufacturing cost reductions, which allow the customer to be offered a price close to what mass production. Customer-centric companies are likely to fill a gap in the global, integrated supply chain, which is already benefiting from economies of scale and a personalized approach to manufacturing and services. Customers will design their products online. An extremely flexible supply chain will produce in "Batch Size 1" (industrial scale unit production) mode in real time based on customer orders, leading to very short production lead times (Senanayake & Little, 2010). The supply of inputs and intermediates will be based on demand forecasts derived from demand. Machines will be designed to minimize changeover times to accommodate changes in demand, batch sizes, specifications and other parameters. Despite the flexibility, the company will still need to ensure very high machine throughput (Fatorachian & Kazemi, 2018).

The increasingly dynamic development of the market means that gaining competitive advantages goes beyond the classic norms of competing on price, availability and quality. The competitiveness of companies that based their strategy solely on the area of production is currently declining, which to some extent is the result of market pressure from consumers who want to participate in the product design process. This is confirmed by the research conducted by Sebastian Saniuk and Sandra Grabowska on social expectations and market changes in the era of Industry 4.0. The main objective of the research was to demonstrate the need to reorganize production management methods in modern enterprises in view of the implementation of the Industry 4.0 concept. The study was conducted on a group of 504 potential customers and consumers representing the Silesian, Lower Silesian, Greater Poland and Lubuskie provinces. Assuming a confidence level of 0.99 and an error of 10%, it was determined that the minimum size of the general population should be 166 customers. Therefore, the information contained in the received surveys can be considered representative. The survey was conducted using the CAWI (Computer Assisted Web Interview) method. The respondents were students (full-time, part-time and postgraduate) and their family members, in various age categories. Most respondents were from large- and medium-sized cities (59%). It is worth noting that the majority of respondents rated their material situation as good (64.1%) and sufficient (23.24%). A very good material situation was declared by about 13.9% of respondents. Only 1.8% of respondents declared a bad material situation. About 52% of respondents were interested in buying personalized products. Most often, such products are purchased by consumers aged 19–25 (38.04%), 26–35 (14.95%), 36–45 (15.76%), rarely by consumers aged 56–67 (7.61%), very rarely such purchases are made by consumers over 67 (1.36%). Based on these results, it can be seen that the most active group of consumers purchasing personalized products are young people aged 19–45.

Of particular note are the types of products that are personalized by respondents. The most common types of personalization are electronics and consumer electronics (42% of respondents), customized food and catering (39% of respondents) and various types of accessories (calendars, cases, pens and so on) (33% of respondents). Consumers are also eager to personalize clothing and footwear, jewelry and children's toys. They are less likely to use personalization when buying cosmetics (17%), cars (15.3%), household appliances and software (12.8%) (Saniuk et al., 2020). The propensity to purchase personalized products by product group (category) is shown in Figure 2.1.

Regarding the level of customer involvement in the personalized product process, respondents expressed different interests in strategies depending on the type of products. Pure customization is the most expected strategy when buying food services (38%), jewelry (42%), furniture and garden equipment (37%), clothes and shoes (44%). "Tailor-made" customization was most often chosen by customers buying furniture and garden equipment (37%), food services (31%), clothes and shoes (31%), car accessories (32%). Standardized customization was indicated most often by respondents when buying electronics (36%), toys (32%), cosmetics (31%), car accessories (30%), common products (30%). In contrast, pure standardization applies to only purchases of common-use products (35%) (Saniuk et al., 2020). Detailed results are shown in Figure 2.2.

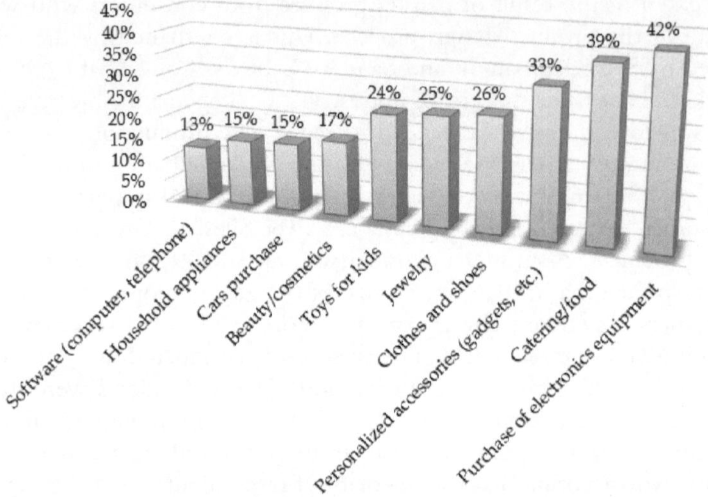

Figure 2.1 Types of products subject to personalization

Source: Authors' elaboration.

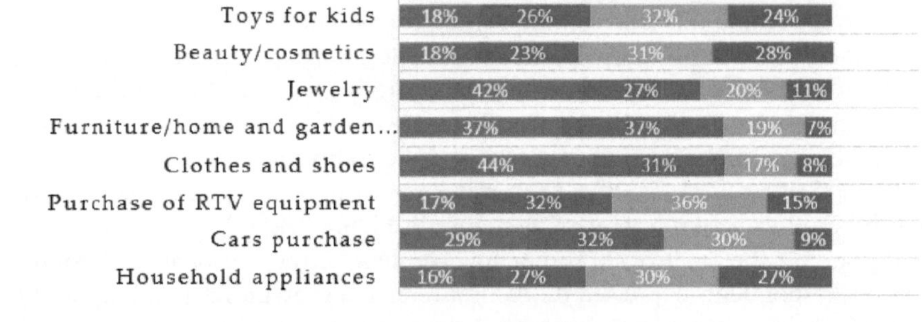

Figure 2.2 Expected customization options for each product group

Source: Authors' elaboration.

One of the reasons for the high interest in personalization is the consumer's emotional involvement in creating a product that will express his preferences and personal expectations. Most often, respondents cited uniqueness (56.2%) as the main reason for purchasing personalized products. Comfort of use (48.1%), the ability to influence the end result of the product (46.1%) and the opportunity to purchase a gift that reflects the characteristics of the recipient (41.9%) were also important reasons. More than 39% of respondents associate the purchase of a personalized product with a guarantee of higher quality. In addition, respondents emphasize the uniqueness of products that better reflects their personality (34.1% of respondents) while indicating that standard products often do not meet their expectations (33.3% of respondents) (Saniuk et al., 2020).

The need for more interaction between the manufacturer and the customer is evidenced by the respondents' opinion regarding their interest in participating in the product design process (29.1% of respondents) (Grabowska & Saniuk, 2022). Figure 2.3 shows the detailed responses of respondents regarding the reasons for their purchase.

As many as 39% of respondents accept a higher price for a personalized product compared to that of a standard offer. Some 58% of respondents make this contingent on the amount of the price difference. Only 3% of respondents are not willing to pay for the opportunity to personalize a product (Grabowska & Saniuk, 2021).

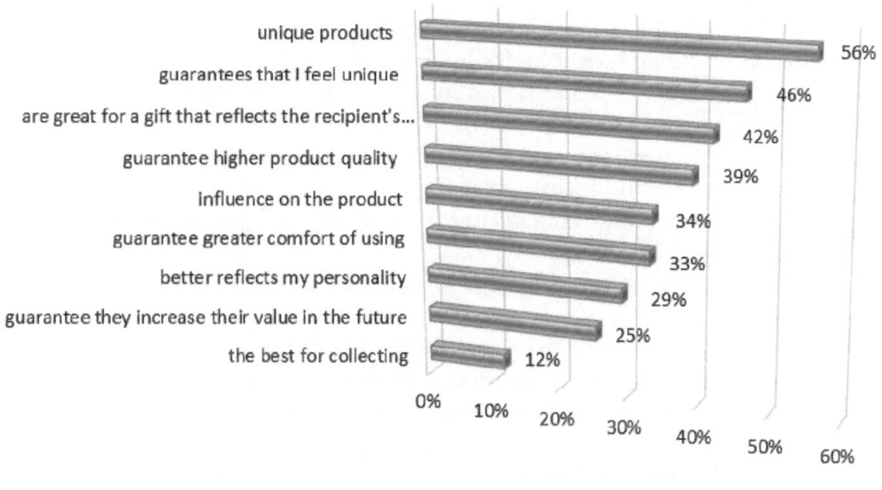

Figure 2.3 Top reasons for buying personalized products

Source: Authors' elaboration.

Modern customers are already accustomed to a lot of choice and the privileged position they are in, they expect more than just the best quality product at the lowest price. Customers expect to be able to personalize products, and this phenomenon is already quite evident in many industries, especially in clothing and footwear, consumer electronics or automotive. Providing personalized products can guarantee benefits for both sides of the transaction. A customer who is satisfied with the product he or she receives will be more loyal, which in turn can translate into revenue stability for the manufacturer. For today's manufacturing companies, this means, the need for changes in the way production is managed, an orientation toward personalized products and a higher level of business networking, which should build a direct relationship with the consumer involving him in the process of designing and manufacturing products preferably using ICT. In the long term, this could mean a shift, especially by small- and medium-sized enterprises, to the servitization of industrial production.

Servitization of industrial production

The demands of today's consumer market for product personalization and the expectation of low prices are forcing companies to change the way they have been operating so far. Above all, a high degree of flexibility in product design and manufacturing is required, dictated by the need to adapt to growing customer expectations. The solution becomes the adoption of a servitization strategy, which in the case of the economy means the growth of the service sector. The development of servitization of the economy is fostered primarily by (Kowalkowski et al., 2017):

- the transfer of certain types of services from manufacturing companies to specialized service companies to rationalize production costs;
- diffusion of digital technologies in production and logistics processes;
- increased competition and regulation of workplace relations including the creation of social and safe working conditions;
- increasing complementarity of goods and services;
- internationalization of sales and supply markets creates demand for services related to market research, tax advice, knowledge of environmental regulations and trade exchanges;
- individualization of needs (personalization of products).

The concept of servitization has been defined by Vandermerwe and Rada as an extended market package offering combining goods, services, support, self-service and knowledge to create added value in the basic product offering (Vandermerwe & Rada, 1988). In the case of manufacturing processes, there is the servitization of industrial production, understood as the reorientation of companies from offering only products for sale to extending their offerings to include resource services and manufacturing systems (product–service systems). Thanks to the use of new technologies and the widespread digitization of economic processes, servitization is becoming an opportunity to build competitive advantages in the industrial production sector, especially for small- and medium-sized enterprises (Baines et al., 2009). The reorganization of industry through the servitization of production allows companies to expand their capabilities and obtain additional value created in the value chain. Therefore, there is no doubt that the development of production system services influences the development of production sectors (Ulbrych, 2016) and the development of narrow specializations and the establishment of permanent or temporary network relationships. Changes in the strategy of production organization, the use of new and smart technologies, often replacing employed workers, contribute to the cooperation of enterprises, the exchange of know-how and the development of production systems services oriented toward closer interaction with the customer. Interest in the role of services in manufacturing continues to grow (Bustinza et al., 2015).

Servitization usually involves enterprises that produce goods to which services are additionally provided. In manufacturing enterprises, servitization involves the development and delivery of new services or complex systems that integrate the goods and services provided (product–service solutions). A manufacturing enterprise shifts from exchanging goods with the customer to providing complex services (solutions) (Rabetino et al., 2017). Often, servitization is equated as combining or surrounding products with services (Kohtamäki et al., 2020).

For manufacturing companies, servitization means a significant change in the way they shape their offerings in the market and how they compete. That is, abandoning a model that focuses on offering a physical product (possibly improving it) and adopting a model that relies on regular services around that product (Baines et al., 2020). The development of ICT networks and business-to-customer systems interaction with the customer is increasingly effective. Rather than focusing solely on product sales and marketing, the modern manufacturer is increasingly adopting a strategy of selling a system of services related to that product.

Servitization requires significant changes in many areas of a company's operations and even requires a change in its business model. Today's product offered to the market should be seen as a platform for providing the services that customers expect. In fact, these solutions are often captured in product–service systems, combinations of products and services. Customers get value from them only if they actually receive the service – hence the concept of value in use (Payne et al., 2021).

Servitization is much easier to implement today thanks to the Fourth Industrial Revolution and the application of new Industry 4.0 technologies. Industry 4.0 pillars such as Industrial Internet of Things, Big Data, cloud computing, augmented reality and commonly used sensors (sensors) in cyber-physical manufacturing systems effectively support the operation of business models based on servitization. The use of new technologies promotes communication between the manufacturer–service provider and the customer using the product. Sensors constantly monitor the state of the product, which promotes rapid response in the event of failure or wear of components, parts of the product. With such a business model, the customer pays not only for the product but also for the service it receives from the supplier. This means a steady stream of revenue over the life of the product. In addition, the manufacturer obtains information to support research and development processes, analyzing the functioning of the product performance, possible failures can improve the product offering. Figure 2.4 shows a diagram of the transformation of a manufacturing company to a production and service company.

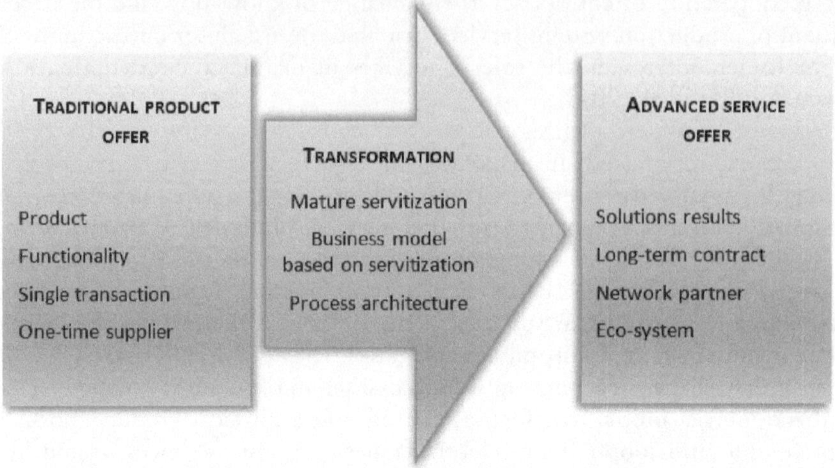

Figure 2.4 Transformation of a manufacturing enterprise

Source: Authors' elaboration.

Servitization can also be understood as a strategy for creating service revenue streams. In this context, we can talk about three levels of services offered by manufacturers (Baines et al., 2009):

- Level I: basic services – goods and spare parts, once they leave the factory, cease to be a problem for the manufacturer, at the same time they also cease to be a source of revenue.
- Level II: intermediate services – product repair, maintenance, overhaul, technical assistance, training, condition monitoring, product maintenance provides manufacturers with a steady source of revenue.
- Level III: advanced services take after-sales services to a higher level of customer interaction and are more relationship- and customer-oriented than just selling and servicing a product. In many cases, advanced services are provided on a subscription model.

Servitization and the company's focus on advanced services aimed at building close customer relationships offer a number of benefits, the most important of which are (Feng et al., 2021):

- better tailoring to customers' needs;
- personalization of products;
- enhanced product innovation;
- additional revenue streams;
- increased customer loyalty;

- increased revenues and profits;
- increased competition in the market.

The achievable benefits of using advanced services in servitization motivates companies to apply new business models based on servitization. Providing advanced services requires the addition of resources and new staff competencies different from those used in ordinary traditional manufacturing. This is even more difficult due to the lack of an established framework for enterprises. Manufacturing companies can offer additional services to complement their traditional products, such as maintenance and fleet maintenance. The development of business networking is also having an effect (Pistoni & Songini, 2017).

Nowadays, companies are focusing on creating interactions between tangible and intangible goods in manufacturing processes. This means, an increase in demand for the creation of production support services that simultaneously improve the productivity and competitiveness of manufacturing enterprises. The range of advanced services offered by modern manufacturing enterprises can also include production systems services (intelligent resources) for networked cooperation (Kamal et al., 2020). These resources are used for the implementation of joint projects with the active participation of the customer, for example, in the creation of new personalized products. This gives birth to another level of development of enterprises operating on the basis of new business models of cyber-physical networks of manufacturing enterprises.

Servitization requires significant changes in many areas of a company's operations and a change in its business model. Today's product should be viewed as a platform for delivering personalized services. A positive effect of personalized production can be an extension of the life cycle of manufactured products and an increase in the level of sustainable production and consumption. This thesis is confirmed by a survey of respondents, who declare a longer life cycle for a personalized product compared to a standardized product (Grabowska & Saniuk, 2022) (Figure 2.2).

As the main reason for the development of servitization should be seen in the qualities that service companies possess, which are characterized by entrepreneurship, flexibility and creativity, and have the ability to quickly adapt to market conditions, search for market niches and establish close contact with customers (Rabetino et al., 2017). It is these qualities that are expected by modern manufacturers looking to meet the expectations of the modern customer. This requires the adoption of a simple organizational structure and the speed of the decision-making process adapted to the actual needs and capabilities of buyers. Today's supply chains are irresistible to disruption, which adds to the problems of business-oriented product manufacturing companies. Chesbrough suggests that entrepreneurs need to stop thinking like manufacturers and start thinking about business from a customer-oriented service perspective (Chesbrough, 2011).

The considerations presented in the chapter indicate an increasing level of interest in production personalization by both consumers and manufacturers.

This increase in consumer interest is due to satisfaction with the long-term use of personalized products and their better fit to their needs. Noteworthy is the increased awareness of the modern consumer and attention to the social responsibility of manufacturers. Social media is creating new behavior based on conscious consumption, the development of sharing economy behavior and care for the environment. This is also due to the strategy of sustainable consumption and production and general awareness of the need to protect the environment and the problem of dwindling natural resources.

There is no doubt that such a profile of the modern consumer has been greatly influenced by the development of the Internet, mobile telephony, market globalization and many other conditions having their roots in the macro environment. In addition, the considerations presented indicate that there is a need to personalize production, especially for more complex products. Today's consumers confirm a high level of satisfaction with having a personalized product and no reason to replace it with another, which can significantly reduce consumption and attachment to a once-purchased product for the long term. High consumer maturity is evidenced by an interest in customer participation, in product development and the development of production customization. A mature consumer wants to buy products tailored to his needs and use them for a long time if they meet his expectations. This is a prerequisite for achieving a higher level of sustainable consumption.

Nowadays, companies will have to change their orientation from product to service in networks and generally expand their product offerings to include services as part of a servitization strategy. This means active interaction with consumers, and the level of product creation is shifted from the perspective of creating only a physical product to creating new experiences and building consumer satisfaction. When buying a personalized product, the customer makes this purchase with greater awareness and feels greater satisfaction with the purchase, which leads to a reduction in the overall level of consumption in the long term and an increase in sustainable consumption (Grabowska & Saniuk, 2021, 2022).

Today, therefore, companies should go beyond the standard exploration of market potential by meeting consumer needs and offer a high level of service oriented to involve the consumer in the process of designing, manufacturing and delivering the product to the customer to satisfy individual preference.

Bibliography

Adamik, A. (2018). Inteligencja organizacji w erze IR 4.0. *Studia i Prace Kolegium Zarządzania i Finansów* (161), 81–97.

Ahrens, D., & Spöttl, G. (2015, June). Industrie 4.0 und Herausforderungen für die Qualifizierung von Fachkräften. In *Digitalisierung industrieller Arbeit* (pp. 184–205). Nomos Verlagsgesellschaft mbH & Co. KG.

Allon, G., & Babich, V. (2020). Crowdsourcing and crowdfunding in the manufacturing and services sectors. *Manufacturing & Service Operations Management*, *22*(1), 102–112.

Anshari, M., Almunawar, M. N., Lim, S. A., & Al-Mudimigh, A. (2019). Customer relationship management and big data enabled: Personalization & customization of services. *Applied Computing and Informatics*, *15*(2), 94–101.

Baines, T. S., Bigdeli, A. Z., Sousa, R., & Schroeder, A. (2020). Framing the servitization transformation process: A model to understand and facilitate the servitization journey. *International Journal of Production Economics*, *221*, 107463.

Baines, T. S., Lightfoot, H. W., Benedettini, O., & Kay, J. M. (2009). The servitization of manufacturing: A review of literature and reflection on future challenges. *Journal of Manufacturing Technology Management*, *20*(5), 547–567.

Bustinza, O. F., Bigdeli, A. Z., Baines, T., & Elliot, C. (2015). Servitization and competitive advantage: The importance of organizational structure and value chain position. *Research-Technology Management*, *58*(5), 53–60.

Caputo, A., Pizzi, S., Pellegrini, M. M., & Dabić, M. (2021). Digitalization and business models: Where are we going? A science map of the field. *Journal of Business Research*, *123*, 489–501.

Chesbrough, H. (2011). The case for open services innovation: The commodity trap. *California Management Review*, *53*(3), 5–20.

Ciechomski, W. (2019). Marka własna detalisty – potencjał rynku i postrzeganie wizerunku. *Przedsiębiorczość i Zarządzanie*, *20*(6.2), 401–411.

Ebert, C., & Duarte, C. H. C. (2018). Digital transformation. *IEEE Software*, *35*(4), 16–21.

Emmelkamp, P. M., & Meyerbröker, K. (2021). Virtual reality therapy in mental health. *Annual Review of Clinical Psychology*, *17*, 495–519.

Fatorachian, H., & Kazemi, H. (2018). A critical investigation of industry 4.0 in manufacturing: Theoretical operationalisation framework. *Production Planning & Control*, *29*(8), 633–644.

Feng, C., Jiang, L., Ma, R., & Bai, C. (2021). Servitization strategy, manufacturing organizations and firm performance: A theoretical framework. *Journal of Business & Industrial Marketing*, *36*, 1909–1928. https://doi.org/10.1108/jbim-04-2020-0184

Ferreira, J. J., Fernandes, C. I., & Ferreira, F. A. (2019). To be or not to be digital, that is the question: Firm innovation and performance. *Journal of Business research*, *101*, 583–590. https://doi.org/10.1016/j.jbusres.2018.11.013

Gajdzik, B., Grabowska, S., & Saniuk, S. (2021, September). Key socio-economic megatrends and trends in the context of the industry 4.0 framework. *Forum Scientiae Oeconomia*, *9*(3), 5–22.

Gobble, M. M. (2018). Digital strategy and digital transformation. *Research-Technology Management*, *61*(5), 66–71.

Grabowska, S., & Saniuk, S. (2021). Modern marketing for customized products under conditions of fourth industrial revolution. In *Industry 4.0* (pp. 159–171). Routledge.

Grabowska, S., & Saniuk, S. (2022). Servitization and the business model of cyber-physical networks in the context of personalized production. *European Research Studies Journal*, *XXV*(1), 955–966.

Gualtieri, L., Rauch, E., & Vidoni, R. (2021). Emerging research fields in safety and ergonomics in industrial collaborative robotics: A systematic literature review. *Robotics and Computer-Integrated Manufacturing*, *67*, 101998.

Haoxiang, W., & Smys, S. (2021). Big data analysis and perturbation using data mining algorithm. *Journal of Soft Computing Paradigm (JSCP)*, *3*(01), 19–28.

Hastig, G. M., & Sodhi, M. S. (2020). Blockchain for supply chain traceability: Business requirements and critical success factors. *Production and Operations Management*, *29*(4), 935–954.

Hermann, M., Pentek, T., & Otto, B. (2016, January). Design principles for industrie 4.0 scenarios. In *2016 49th Hawaii international conference on system sciences (HICSS)* (pp. 3928–3937). IEEE.

Huawei. (2021). *Intelligent world 2030*. https://www-file.huawei.com/-/media/corp2020/pdf/giv/intelligent_world_2030_en.pdf

Iglesias, O., Markovic, S., Bagherzadeh, M., & Singh, J. J. (2020). Co-creation: A key link between corporate social responsibility, customer trust, and customer loyalty. *Journal of Business Ethics*, *163*(1), 151–166.

Jahani, N., Sepehri, A., Vandchali, H. R., & Tirkolaee, E. B. (2021). Application of Industry 4.0 in the procurement processes of supply chains: A systematic literature review. *Sustainability*, *13*(14), 7520.

Javaid, M., Haleem, A., Singh, R. P., Khan, S., & Suman, R. (2021). Blockchain technology applications for industry 4.0: A literature-based review. *Blockchain: Research and Applications*, 100027.

Kamal, M. M., Sivarajah, U., Bigdeli, A. Z., Missi, F., & Koliousis, Y. (2020). Servitization implementation in the manufacturing organisations: Classification of strategies, definitions, benefits and challenges. *International Journal of Information Management*, *55*, 102206.

Kaplan, A. M., & Haenlein, M. (2006). Toward a parsimonious definition of traditional and electronic mass customization. *Journal of Product Innovation Management*, *23*(2), 168–182.

Kohtamäki, M., Parida, V., Patel, P. C., & Gebauer, H. (2020). The relationship between digitalization and servitization: The role of servitization in capturing the financial potential of digitalization. *Technological Forecasting and Social Change*, *151*, 119804.

Koren, Y., Shpitalni, M., Gu, P., & Hu, S. J. (2015). Product design for mass-individualization. *Procedia Cirp*, *36*, 64–71.

Kowalkowski, C., Gebauer, H., Kamp, B., & Parry, G. (2017). Servitization and deservitization: Overview, concepts, and definitions. *Industrial Marketing Management*, *60*, 4–10.

Kumar, A. (2007). From mass customization to mass personalization: A strategic transformation. *International Journal of Flexible Manufacturing Systems*, *19*(4), 533–547.

Lampel, J., & Mintzberg, H. (1996). Customizing customization. *Sloan Management Review*, *38*(1), 21–30.

Mintzberg, H., Ghoshal, S., Lampel, J., & Quinn, J. B. (2003). *The strategy process: Concepts, contexts, cases*. Pearson Education.

Młody, M. (2018). Personalizacja produktów a Przemysł 4.0 – ocena słuszności implementacji nowoczesnych technologii w przemyśle produkcyjnym z perspektywy konsumentów. *Ekonomika i Organizacja Przedsiębiorstw*, 62–72.

Newell, F. (1997). *The new rules of marketing: How to use one-to-one relationship marketing to be the leader in your industry*. Irwin Professional Publishing.

Nguyen, D. C., Ding, M., Pathirana, P. N., Seneviratne, A., Li, J., & Poor, H. V. (2021). Federated learning for internet of things: A comprehensive survey. *IEEE Communications Surveys & Tutorials*, *23*(3), 1622–1658.

Pallant, J. L., Sands, S., & Karpen, I. O. (2020). The 4Cs of mass customization in service industries: A customer lens. *Journal of Services Marketing*, *34*, 499–511. https://doi.org/10.1108/jsm-04-2019-0176

Pape, S., & Rannenberg, K. (2019). Applying privacy patterns to the internet of things'(IoT) architecture. *Mobile Networks and Applications*, *24*(3), 925–933.

Payne, E. H. M., Dahl, A. J., & Peltier, J. (2021). Digital servitization value co-creation framework for AI services: A research agenda for digital transformation in financial service ecosystems. *Journal of Research in Interactive Marketing*, *15*, 200–222. https://doi.org/10.1108/jrim-12-2020-0252

Pistoni, A., & Songini, L. (2017). *Servitization strategy and managerial control*. Emerald Group Publishing.

Pivoto, D. G., de Almeida, L. F., da Rosa Righi, R., Rodrigues, J. J., Lugli, A. B., & Alberti, A. M. (2021). Cyber-physical systems architectures for industrial internet of things applications in industry 4.0: A literature review. *Journal of Manufacturing Systems, 58*, 176–192.

Quayyum, F., Cruzes, D. S., & Jaccheri, L. (2021). Cybersecurity awareness for children: A systematic literature review. *International Journal of Child-Computer Interaction, 30*, 100343.

Rabetino, R., Kohtamäki, M., & Gebauer, H. (2017). Strategy map of servitization. *International Journal of Production Economics, 192*, 144–156.

Rachinger, M., Rauter, R., Müller, C., Vorraber, W., & Schirgi, E. (2018). Digitalization and its influence on business model innovation. *Journal of Manufacturing Technology Management, 30*(8), 1143–1160. https://doi.org/10.1108/JMTM-01-2018-0020

Saberi, S., Kouhizadeh, M., Sarkis, J., & Shen, L. (2019). Blockchain technology and its relationships to sustainable supply chain management. *International Journal of Production Research, 57*(7), 2117–2135.

Sadeeq, M. M., Abdulkareem, N. M., Zeebaree, S. R., Ahmed, D. M., Sami, A. S., & Zebari, R. R. (2021). IoT and cloud computing issues, challenges and opportunities: A review. *Qubahan Academic Journal, 1*(2), 1–7.

Saniuk, S., Grabowska, S., & Gajdzik, B. (2020). Personalization of products in the industry 4.0 concept and its impact on achieving a higher level of sustainable consumption. *Energies, 13*(22), 5895.

Semeraro, C., Lezoche, M., Panetto, H., & Dassisti, M. (2021). Digital twin paradigm: A systematic literature review. *Computers in Industry, 130*, 103469.

Senanayake, M. M., & Little, T. J. (2010). Mass customization: Points and extent of apparel customization. *Journal of Fashion Marketing and Management: An International Journal, 14*(2), 282–299.

Sommer, M., Stjepandić, J., & Stobrawa, S. (2021). Incremental update of a digital twin of a production system by using scan and object recognition. In *Transdisciplinary engineering for resilience: Responding to system disruptions* (pp. 83–92). IOS Press.

Szymkowiak, A. (2014). E-kastomizacja produktów – wykorzystanie narzędzi online w e-commerce. *Marketing i Rynek, 8*, 933–938.

Torn, I. A. R., & Vaneker, T. H. (2019). Mass personalization with industry 4.0 by SMEs: A concept for collaborative networks. *Procedia Manufacturing, 28*, 135–141.

Ulbrych, M. (2016). Serwicyzacja produkcji przemysłowej. Wnioski dla Polski. *Finanse, Rynki Finansowe, Ubezpieczenia, 81*, 255–264.

Vandermerwe, S., & Rada, J. (1988). Servitization of business: Adding value by adding services. *European Management Journal, 6*(4), 314–324.

Vesanen, J. (2007). What is personalization? A conceptual framework. *European Journal of Marketing, 41*, 409–418. https://doi.org/10.1108/03090560710737534

Windelband, L. (2014). Zukunft der Facharbeit im Zeitalter "Industrie 4.0". *Journal of Technical Education (JOTED), 2*(2).

Zhang, C., & Lu, Y. (2021). Study on artificial intelligence: The state of the art and future prospects. *Journal of Industrial Information Integration, 23*, 100224.

Zhou, K., Liu, T., & Zhou, L. (2015, August). Industry 4.0: Towards future industrial opportunities and challenges. In *2015 12th International conference on fuzzy systems and knowledge discovery (FSKD)* (pp. 2147–2152). IEEE.

3 The Fourth Industrial Revolution as a new environment for business models

Fourth Industrial Revolution – Industry 4.0

The Fourth Industrial Revolution refers to the social, industrial and technological changes brought about by the digital transformation of industry, which are identified with the concept of Industry 4.0. It can be defined as an age in which modern technological solutions shape the industrial environment and affect the economy and society, influencing the intensification of sustainable global development (Grabowska & Saniuk, 2022a). The new concept of industry was widely adopted in Europe in the second half of the 21st century and was forged during the work initiated by the German government in 2010 on identifying and analyzing upcoming disruptive changes of strategic importance to the German economy. At the 2011 Hannover Fair, the term was used for the first time, during presentations on the future of industry. The work of a working group of representatives from German business, industry and academia resulted in a document published in 2013, outlining recommendations for the implementation of a program called the "Industry 4.0 strategic initiative," which presented a picture of a new cyber-physical reality shaped by revolutionary changes in industry. The term Industry 4.0 was also used in the German government's draft technology development strategy "High-Tech Strategy 2020." One of the key areas of this strategy is defined as: "Digital Economy and Society" (Müller et al., 2018). The Bosch factory in Germany is considered to be a forerunner of change on practical grounds. In the literature, Industry 4.0 is defined in terms of many perspectives (Table 3.1), but there is still no universally accepted unambiguous definition of Industry 4.0.

Based on these definitions, several of its advantages can be defined: increased economic efficiency, increased labor productivity, flexibility, reduced production costs and increased return on investment. It is worth noting the modification of the relationship between human capital and technological capital. Automation of technological capital translates into high-quality products and services. Increased productivity is achieved primarily through automated or semi-automated decision-making. Production is monitored and it is much easier to bring new products to the production line and create opportunities for a single production operation. Production is flexible and the factory is smart (Gajdzik & Grabowska, 2018).

DOI: 10.4324/9781003317401-4

Table 3.1 Example definitions of Industry 4.0

Source/Author	*Definition*
High-Tech Strategy 2020	Shifting the smart manufacturing and production paradigm from centralized to decentralized. Smart manufacturing is becoming the norm in a world where smart machines, systems and networks are able to independently exchange and respond to information to manage industrial production processes.
McKinsey	The next phase of digitization in the manufacturing sector is driven by four disruptions: 1 Staggering growth in data, computing power and connectivity, especially new low-power wide area networks; 2 The emergence of analytics and business intelligence capabilities; 3 New forms of human–machine interaction, such as touch interfaces and augmented reality systems; 4 Improvements in the transmission of digital data instructions for the physical world, such as advanced robotics and 3D printing.
The Industrial Internet Consortium	Integration of complex physical machines and devices with networked sensors and software to predict, control and plan for better economic and social outcomes.
Boston Consulting Group (BCG)	New digital industrial technology that is driven by nine fundamental technological advances: Big Data and Analytics, simulation, autonomous robots, horizontal and vertical, systems integration, industrial Internet of Things, cybersecurity, cloud with data, additive manufacturing, augmented reality.
Merkel, OECD Conference (2014)	Comprehensive transformation of the entire industrial and manufacturing sphere by combining digital technology and the Internet with conventional industry. In short, everything in and around manufacturing operations (suppliers, plants, distributors, even the products themselves) is digitally connected, providing a highly integrated value chain.
Brettel et al. (2014)	Digitization of production and processes through increased intelligence. It focuses on creating intelligent products and production processes.
Schmidt et al. (2015)	Integrating smart products into digital and physical processes.
Toro et al. (2015)	Integrating complex machinery and equipment, with sensors and software networks, to predict, control and improve business plans.
Hermann et al. (2016)	A holistic system of information technology, people, machines and tools in which cyber-physical systems (CPS) monitor physical processes, creating a virtual copy of the physical world and making it decentralized for decision-making.
Sanders et al. (2016)	Industrial revolution using the Internet and future technologies and intelligent systems with enhanced human capabilities and machine interaction paradigms.
Qin et al. (2016)	A manufacturing concept that relies on the exchange of information and control of machines and production units operating autonomously and intelligently in an interoperable environment.

(*Continued*)

Table 3.1 (Continued)

Source/Author	*Definition*
Zhong et al. (2017)	The holistic system combines embedded manufacturing system technologies with intelligent manufacturing processes to pave the way for a new technological era that will fundamentally change industry value, manufacturing value chains and business models.
Santos et al. (2017)	A comprehensive concept, as well as a new trend in manufacturing, based on the integration of a set of technologies that enable smart ecosystems.
Wortmann et al. (2017)	A vision of manufacturing in which intelligent, interconnected production optimizes the complete value-added chain to reduce costs and time to market. This is the smart factory of the future, the successful implementation of which requires solving problems from multiple domains.
J. Lu (2017)	An integrated, customized, optimized, service-oriented and interoperable manufacturing process correlated with algorithms, Big Data and advanced technologies.

Source: Based on Janik, A., & Ryszko, A. (2018, November). Mapping the field of Industry 4.0 based on bibliometric analysis. *International Business Information Management Association Conference (IBIMA), 32.*

All definitions refer to solutions of an innovative nature and emphasize the need to implement them in modern companies. Such implementation, however, requires knowledge from many fields. Today, the number of companies implementing Industry 4.0 solutions is growing. These are companies in various industries producing equipment, furnishings, machinery, automobiles and services. For the first time in the history of mankind, technology, connecting an increasing number of industries with society, makes it possible to influence the volume and quality of production, as well as the functionality of products. Industry 4.0 introduces leading-edge IT solutions in all aspects of production, making it possible to create not only specific products ordered by customers but also entire related value chains (Maresova et al., 2018). Through the use of advanced ICT, it is possible to tailor production more precisely to customers' expectations while maintaining low costs, high quality and efficiency (Longo et al., 2017; Müller, 2018). New business models and technologies, such as AI or additive manufacturing, are accelerating industry transformation processes, changing current business methods and market structure. All these artifacts pose new challenges for many areas of management, which must adapt to the digital architecture of the world (Imran, 2018).

Industry 4.0 is an upheaval in manufacturing control methodologies, involving, among other things, dynamic machine changeovers initiated by information carried in workpieces. Communication in Industry 4.0 at the factory level requires broadband communication, including at the level of individual device sensors and actuators in real time and in wide-area network environments. New solutions implemented in factories resulting in changing management paradigms and building new business models based on balancing technology development with quality of life. The changes that are taking place in Industry 4.0 include a wide range of innovations at the level of plants and factories belonging to various industries and services, as well as the functioning of entire societies (Chrzanowski & Glazewska, 2016).

Industry 4.0 refers to the integration of intelligent machines and systems and the introduction of changes in production processes aimed at increasing production efficiency and introducing the possibility of flexible changes in scope. Industry 4.0 is not only about technology, but also about new ways of working and the role of people in industry (Lasi et al., 2014; Ghobakhloo, 2020). Industry 4.0 is a subset of the fourth industrial revolution. Customers and business partners are directly involved in business processes and value creation. Production is coupled with high-quality services. In the future, through intelligent monitoring and decision-making, companies and their entire networks should be able to control and optimize their operations almost in real time (Olsen & Tomlin, 2020).

Industry 4.0 can also be defined in terms of cyber-physical systems, the Internet of Things, the Internet as a Service and the Smart Factory. Six design principles have been proposed that can support companies in implementing Industry 4.0 solutions. These are (Hermann et al., 2015):

- Interoperability – the ability of systems and employees in an enterprise to communicate, exchange data and coordinate activities.
- Virtualization – is associated with monitoring physical processes using a single virtual resource from multiple physical resources or multiple virtual resources from a single physical resource.
- Decentralization – it refers to moving to multiple systems instead of a central system to reduce risk and provide flexibility in operations.
- Real-time virtual capability – Real-time processing capability refers to the collation and processing of data in real time that allows for informed and timely decision-making.
- Service orientation and modularity – The ability to use Big Data Analytics to produce predictive analytics that can help better understand customer needs is referred to as service orientation.
- Modularity – it refers to the ability of companies to flexibly adapt to changing industry demands and needs.

Analyzing publications in the field of Industry 4.0, it is possible to distinguish between several basic technologies of this revolution. These are the following:

- Additive manufacturing (3D design, prototyping, low-volume manufacturing),
- Advanced simulation,
- Autonomous systems
- Big Data Analysis,

- Cloud computing,
- Cognitive computing,
- Cybersecurity,
- Cyber-physical systems,
- Industrial Internet,
- Internet of Everything,
- Internet of Things,
- Internet of Things for the manufacturing industry,
- Manufacturing 4.0,
- Smart Factory,
- Smart manufacturing,
- The connected enterprise.

It can be seen that the aforementioned pillars of Industry 4.0 interpenetrate each other and interact logically, which in the long run will be controlled by AI. The common denominator of these is "digital," which is the basis for the development of Industry 4.0. Moreover, the Internet itself takes on two meanings. In a narrow sense, it is about the Internet with social networks and applications on mobile devices. In a broad sense, it is about the role of the Internet in creating new opportunities for manufacturers, employees and customers (Erboz, 2017). The network includes customers, producers, competitors and suppliers, and their cooperation creates a global space of diverse opportunities. These developments span different areas of cooperation and are unlimited in time and space (Machado et al., 2020). Based on the pillars of Industry 4.0, nine key technologies of Industry 4.0 can be distinguished, as shown in Table 3.2.

In terms of topics in the Industry 4.0 area, much attention is being paid to aspects of sustainability – the consumer, business models, the economy. From the point of view of sustainability, Stock and Selinger (2016) defined Industry 4.0 as a step toward more sustainable industrial value creation, arguing that industrial value creation must be focused on sustainability and Industry 4.0 providing great opportunities to realize sustainable production. By providing detailed information on every point of production (García-Muiña et al., 2020), processes, resources and energy consumption can be optimized across the value network (Gabriel & Pessel, 2016). The new technological solutions promoted by Industry 4.0 should help increase both the efficiency of production and also the environmental performance of products throughout their life cycle. This moreover implies an increase in demand for smart products and smart manufacturing technologies. In a sustainable market, customers (consumers) should make informed choices, buying "environmentally friendly" products, that is, those that are recycled, serviced, renewable, shared and so on. The Fourth Industrial (technological) Revolution has expanded the boundaries of what companies can provide as value to customers. In today's highly competitive manufacturing environment, companies face the challenge of dealing with large data sets, the need to make quick decisions and the flexibility of

Table 3.2 Key technologies of Industry 4.0

No.	*Name*	*Description*
1	Additive Manufacturing	Is a term that covers several methods that enable 3D manufacturing of products by layering one on top of the other. The first additive manufacturing, also known as incremental manufacturing, was developed in the 1980s, and since then the number, functionality and applicability of these processes have grown significantly in the manufacturing sector. Additive Manufacturing can produce complex geometries, reduce manufacturing costs and produce parts from the highest quality materials with small production runs and short lead times. Additive Manufacturing enables the following: advanced part designs, multi-functional parts, parts with multiple materials and consolidation of parts that are difficult to machine. Additive Manufacturing is widely used in several manufacturing sectors, including aerospace, automotive, construction, medical and so on (Bandyopadhyay et al., 2022).
2	Augmented reality	It's a system that makes it possible to connect the real world with the virtual world. The technology allows virtual elements to be superimposed on what can be observed in front of you. Augmented reality is an interactive experience in a real-world environment in which objects in the real world are enhanced by computer-generated perceptual information, sometimes at multiple sensory levels, including visual, auditory, somatosensory and olfactory. Augmented reality can be defined as a system that fulfils three characteristics: a combination of real and virtual worlds, real-time interaction and accurate 3D registration of virtual and real objects. The superimposed sensory information can be constructive (additive to the natural environment) or destructive (mask the natural environment). The experience is seamlessly interwoven with the physical world in such a way that it is perceived as an immersive aspect of the real environment. In this way, augmented reality alters current perceptions of the real environment, while virtual reality completely replaces the real environment (Xiong et al., 2021).
3	Autonomous robots	A key component of Industry 4.0 and is widely used in industrial production. An autonomous robot is characterized by a certain degree of autonomy in perception and action and can independently respond to external stimuli. A typical robot offers many benefits to humans employed in manufacturing companies. It performs tedious, repetitive tasks that are often dangerous and time-consuming. It features high accuracy, increased productivity, reduced errors and long working hours, as there is no need for breaks. The autonomous robot adds to this list of benefits the ability to incorporate machine learning, meaning that it makes its own decisions based on programming (Aubin et al., 2022).
4	Big Data	The ability to collect, store and analyze huge amounts of data, the analysis of which can be used to identify inefficiencies and production bottlenecks, optimize production quality, save energy and improve service and equipment diagnostics. In the context of Industry 4.0, the collection and comprehensive evaluation of data from a wide variety of sources – production equipment and systems, as well as business and customer management systems – will become the standard to support real-time decision-making (Naeem et al., 2022).

(*Continued*)

Table 3.2 (Continued)

No.	*Name*	*Description*
5	Cloud computing	Large data sets are now being shared in the cloud. Companies are already using cloud-based software for some corporate applications and analytics, but with Industry 4.0, more manufacturing-related businesses will require more data sharing on company websites and intranets. At the same time, the performance of cloud technology will improve, reaching response times of just a few milliseconds. As a result, machine data and functionality will increasingly be deployed in the cloud, enabling more data-driven services for manufacturing systems. Even systems that monitor and control processes can rely on the cloud. This is where security plays an important role (Javadpour et al., 2022).
6	Industrial Internet of Things	It is the interconnected networking of sensors, instruments and other devices together with industrial applications of computers, including manufacturing and energy management. This connectivity allows for the collection, exchange and analysis of data, potentially facilitating improvements in productivity and efficiency, as well as other economic benefits. Industrial Internet of Things is an evolution of distributed control system (DCS) that allows for a higher degree of automation by using cloud computing to improve and optimize process control (Serror et al., 2020).
7	Simulation	This approximation based on established mathematical models or statistical tools shows the behaviour of a product or process through graphics. Simulations provide users with the freedom to experiment under different conditions and observe the results to make informed decisions. However, there is a need to verify simulations with an acceptable percentage of error for use in real-world scenarios in the program. Three-dimensional simulations of products, materials and manufacturing processes are used in the design phase. Simulations can use real-time data to reflect the physical world in a virtual model that can include machines, products and people. This allows operators to test and optimize machine settings for the next product in the virtual world before the physical switchover, thereby reducing machine setup time and improving quality (Xiong et al., 2021).
8	Systems integration	Vertical and horizontal integration and data exchange of companies, raw material and equipment suppliers and customers. Most of today's IT systems are not fully integrated. Participants in processes are rarely closely interconnected. This also applies to production and service departments or the shop floor, whose functions and activities are not integrated. However, with Industry 4.0, companies, departments, functions and capabilities will become more cohesive as IT platforms, universal data integration networks evolve to manage the complex task of exchanging product and production data between multiple partners (Imam et al., 2022).
9	Technologies to support cybersecurity	Cybersecurity is the practice of protecting systems, networks and programs from digital attacks. Cyberattacks are typically aimed at accessing, altering or destroying sensitive information, defrauding users or disrupting normal business processes. Implementing effective cybersecurity measures is particularly challenging today, as there are more devices than people, and attackers are becoming increasingly innovative. The shift to digitization, cyber-physical systems (CPS), connected devices and real-time communications in the context of Industry 4.0 is shedding new light on the data generated and the need to protect it. Cybersecurity (CS) is quickly becoming a major concern for manufacturers and consumers (Haleem et al., 2022).

Source: Own study.

manufacturing processes (Rojko, 2017). The modern nature of manufacturing is being shaped by a paradigm shift from mass production to unit and batch production oriented toward meeting customer needs and providing customized products. The range of customer expectations of products is very wide and diverse (Donnellyet al., 2015).

In the media and literature, one can still see the prevailing view that Industry 4.0 is only technological changes that should be implemented in manufacturing companies, yet this industrial revolution, its trends and effects are visible in all macro and micro areas of the market. The proposed technological changes, which have gained strategic importance in the thinking and actions of many market participants, while penetrating all links in the value chain and the ways in which they are connected, have changed the scope of competition and the way consumer needs are met. At the same time, there are dynamic and clear changes in the needs and expectations of modern consumers. Therefore, the authors propose to define the Fourth Industrial Revolution as the age in which modern technological solutions shape the industrial environment and affect the economy and society, influencing the intensification of sustainable global development while Industry 4.0 as the modern, technological and information environment of the enterprise. The pillars of Industry 4.0 are autonomous robots, big data, cloud computing, systems integration, additive manufacturing, the industrial Internet of Things, augmented reality, simulation and technologies supporting cybersecurity (Grabowska & Saniuk, 2022).

Smart factories of the future

The development of modern technologies covers almost every sector of the economy and actively supports entrepreneurs as well. Thanks to the improvements introduced, automation of some processes or improved communication between various departments in companies, it is possible to provide services at an even higher level and, most importantly, in a shorter time and at lower cost. These issues also apply to factories. With Industry 4.0 technology, everything becomes possible (Shi et al., 2020).

A Smart Factory can be defined as an enterprise in which cyber-physical systems control physical processes, create virtual copies of the real world and make decentralized decisions and through the industrial Internet of Things, communicate and collaborate with each other and with people in real time. Meanwhile, through cloud computing, internal and inter-operational services are offered and used (Grabowska, 2020).

The concept of a Smart Factory refers to the application of modern robotization techniques and digital systems that enable efficient management of industrial production. Each Smart Factory has an enormous amount of data from sensors embedded in both machines and software that coordinates internal and external processes. This makes it possible to increase production efficiency while reducing the need for constant supervision by personnel. The most advanced factories of this type need to adjust production volumes to fluctuations in demand, respond to rapid changes in the supply chain and correct process irregularities to avoid downtime. This is done by using, among other things, big data, technology based on processing a large set of data (Big Data), IIoT (Industrial Internet of Things) and simulation techniques, such as using digital twins (Mabkhot et al., 2018; Büchi et al., 2020).

Smart Factories are playing an increasingly important role in the broader supply chain. Rapid technological advances, competitive pressures and the dispersion of demand and globalization of production have accelerated the transformation of factories, which are becoming smarter every year thanks to automation and digitization (Chen et al., 2017).

Analyzing the results of a survey on Smart Factories conducted by Deloitte and MAPI (Manufacturer's Alliance for Productivity and Innovation), up to 86% of manufacturers believe that the evolution toward Smart Factories will be crucial to improving competitiveness (Deloite and MAPI Smart Factory Study, 2019).

There are four general emerging categories of next-generation factories that leverage different pillars of Industry 4.0, but with different emphasis depending on the demand segment and needs they address (McKinsey, 2015):

- Digital mass-individualization factories, otherwise known as customer-centric plants;
- E-plants in a box or mobile modular factories;
- Handmade with digital touch or handmade production strongly supported by digitization;
- Smart-automated and robotized plants.

Mobile modular factories, that is mobile production facilities, can be moved from place to place. Mobility means that such a factory can be flexibly built, commissioned, packaged and moved. Reasons for portability can be market trends, access to raw materials or industry standards.

Both Intelligent Automated and Robotic Factories and Digital Mass Customization Factories require large capital expenditures and yet require high-enough production volumes and therefore high-enough demand that the investments can pay off. The problem is, how to deal with niche subscales and distant markets, such as the growing but highly fragmented African markets?

A mobile modular factory, otherwise known as an "E-plant in a box," bolstered by Industry 4.0 levers such as 3D printing, manufacturing machine flexibility, is a low-capitalization installation and can be quickly configured in new locations at competitive costs. Typically, factories in this archetype take on minimal size and small scale. Factories are able to produce a certain amount of products anywhere on short notice, either on the shop floor or directly on the shop floor, for the duration of the order (Rauch et al., 2015).

Factories can potentially be delivered in containers. In the final version, the e-plant in a box could serve passing customers who stop to design their own product, on site, with the help of specialists. They could choose designs and materials, use simulation tools, and then return to the plant for their product. The plant will thus be very adaptable to local trends due to its proximity to customers and the local ecosystem, and what's more, the time to market will also be reduced due to the proximity of suppliers and customers. The plant may be only slightly automated, but operators will use Industry 4.0 technologies to facilitate their production. An exoskeleton, using human–robot collaboration, for example, could relieve workers of heavy loads, as well as being a lightweight and relatively inexpensive tool. Another example of technology that facilitates work in mobile factories is a flexible manufacturing system with robots operating in a "plug and play" system, performing specific tasks where robot participation would give the greatest benefit. 3D printing can be used to produce spare and custom parts, reducing needed inventory while lowering transportation costs and bypassing import duties on raw materials or semifinished products (Ghondaghsaz & Engesser, 2021).

Customer analysis takes place through a comprehensive end-to-end information flow. Highly skilled central teams support process improvement, design and maintenance. Finally, the mobile manufacturing plant is integrated into the surrounding ecosystem, for example, it produces its own energy, so it doesn't need to be in an industrial zone. It can be located near shopping centers and other locations convenient for customers.

An example of such a mobile manufacturing plant could be mini factories that produce tools and components for large construction projects. They can be located directly in the neighborhood or on a construction site.

A more advanced factory was presented by Nestlé in cooperation with Concept Consult Architects; it is a modular dairy. The design of a new type of modular factory created by Swiss food manufacturer Nestlé can be built in half the time of a traditional factory, up to 50% to 60% of the cost. Unique in terms of the value chain, the concept is based on Industry 4.0 principles and is fully modular and decentralized. Standardized building construction elements have been proposed. Solar panels for heating water and generating electricity, ready-made room equipment in the form of canteens, halls and so on. Standardization enables standardization in the design and construction of industrial plants in countries that lack industrial infrastructure. In these countries, the concept will help the company quickly leave its mark and create local jobs, bringing them closer to customers and raw materials. The modular factory concept has so far been developed to industrialize simple processes, such as repackaging and mixing dry products (such as bouillon cubes), instead of creating more complex products (Sjödin et al., 2018).

Smart automated and robotic factories responding to the demand for mass products specialize in realizing very high production volumes at low costs (lower than the competition), thanks to fully automated and digitized processes. Production in such a factory is carried out on dedicated production lines with common modules for packaging goods (i.e., the activities of portioning and packing products into containers, packages, shipping kits or retail sales). Such a model can be adopted, for example, by food factories that base their business on cooperation with discount chains, where cost competitiveness is very important.

The supply chain in such a factory will be comprehensively integrated, that is, it will be implemented in an end-to-end system (a system created by connecting all logistics and supply chain processes, starting with the customer and going upstream through production to our supplier base, and the flows are bidirectional). Such a model will enable full transparency and optimization of the digital thread, resulting in automated and usually uninterrupted processes and efficient material flows. In addition, robots, which already have the potential to significantly increase operational efficiency, will feature not only higher intelligence but also greater collaboration and safety. Going further, better cooperation between humans and robots will enable operators to work more safely alongside robots on the shop floor. The plant will provide a very high productivity rate per machine by being able to use predictive maintenance to reduce unplanned downtime and optimize throughput in real time. Finished products from a smart automated factory can go to the mass market, while semi-finished products can be the raw material for individualized customer-oriented factories or mobile modular factories (Siegert et al., 2020).

The BMW i3 production plant in Leipzig, Germany, can be considered an early example of the archetype of the smart, automated and robotic factory, as it features a high level of integration and automation at production sites. Robots do their work at every stage of production, including the body shop, paint shop and assembly plant. Real-time tracking and locating of unfinished product is done using RFID technology, and operators have mobile control tablets to monitor and access all necessary data. Finally, factory management is centralized in one main building, which acts as a "central nervous system" (Thoben et al., 2017).

Digital mass-individualized factories focus on high-volume or medium-volume production, but unlike the previous model, they allow full personalization of their products, making them highly individualized. Such products include, for example, automobiles, clothing, footwear, furniture, gates and decorative structural elements. Production lines are technologically and process-ready for short or very short runs, the occurrence of frequent changeovers and personalization of products that differ in color, additional equipment and texture. Production nests often take the form of universal modules. Modularization of the production system is based on machines that adapt to different activities and are able to communicate with each other via the Internet. Modular production nests increase the possibilities for production customization, reduce machine changeover times and increase product personalization to meet all customer requirements and mass customization trends. In this case, the flow of the production sequence is controlled by the product. This means that the product "decides" which slots to use to leave the production line in the shortest possible time (Weking et al., 2020).

Demand for retail products will evolve over time, driven by the strong trend toward increasing product personalization. How can you serve so many customers within the so-called Segment of One? A broad approach to marketing and engaging customers with basic segmentation is no longer an effective way to connect with a new generation of consumers. Customer expectations have increased significantly, which means marketers need to innovate by finding new ways to understand and encourage their customers. "Segment of One," literally translated as "Segment of One," means changing the way customers are segmented. To be successful, companies need to see their customers as individuals rather than assigning them to general demographic categories. Basic segmentation is no longer sufficient, as customers have come to expect a deeper connection with their favorite brands. Putting people first requires marketing to use information gathered from historical customer data (e.g., their preferences, search history on a manufacturer's website, and so on) to gain a deep understanding of the complex nature of the consumer and clarity on where a brand should be present to gain the most value (Lee, 2022).

"Customer-centric betting" is likely to fill a gap in the global, integrated supply chain, which is already benefiting from economies of scale and a personalized approach to production and service. Customers will design their products online, and the flexibility of product routing means that designed models will be shipped directly to the most appropriate factory once an order is placed. The extremely flexible supply chain will produce in "Batch Size 1" (industrial-scale unit production) mode in real time based on customer orders, leading to very short lead times. Deliveries of input materials and semifinished products will be based on demand forecasts. Machines will be designed to minimize changeover times to accommodate changes in demand, batch sizes, specifications and other parameters. Despite the flexibility, the plant will still need to ensure that each machine has a very high capacity (Yilmaz, 2021).

An example of a modern company with massively customized factories is Adidas. On the manufacturer's website, customers can design shoes in their own style. The modification begins with the selection of a basic shoe model, along with its type. Then the site user selects one of a wide range of colors, visual embellishments of the shoe (e.g., reflectors, colored inserts, lettering), type of material, type of sole and additional accessories to order (cork keys, overlays, laces). The whole process of modifying the basic shoe model allows you to create your dream configuration according to your own taste, according to your expectations, and to have a product that is not available in the mass offer. This solution allows customers (for an additional fee) to choose such variants of the product, which are missing from the offer of predefined models by the designer (Sudhoff et al., 2020).

The idea of handmade production using digitization applies to products of very high quality, created in unit quantities. These can be goods located in a niche market segment (e.g., aeronautics, military) and also luxury goods (e.g., luxury cars). Factories using digitized craft production employ top-class workers who, being professionals, are able to combine manual labor with modern tools and technologies. Specialists in material processing carry out individual customer orders. The use of the latest technology in this type of factories allows to increase the safety of work, the elements of this technology can replace the manual process at a certain stage of the production process, where a person is much less effective than a robot or the performed activity can endanger human health, an example is a robotic paint shop in factories of the automotive industry. Technological support greatly facilitates the organization of work and the flow of information, thereby reducing production time and maintaining the highest quality of the product to satisfy even the most demanding customers (McKinsey, 2015).

Each of the archetypes of the modern factory has unique characteristics that allow them to be distinguished by their mode of production, but the common and central interest of each enterprise is customer satisfaction. Every factory should interact with the customer to a greater or lesser extent, strive to exchange information and increase trust in the company and enable simple ways to order the desired product, which is greatly facilitated by the Internet of Things (Lehmann et al., 2021). Other common issues that apply to each archetype of a modern factory are:

- competence development and training of managers, line workers and engineers;
- attention to operational perfection and continuous improvement;
- development of digital networks and information flow infrastructure;
- ensuring the cybersecurity of the entire company through the use of appropriate security policies and tools.

Smart Factories are a huge step forward in managing production processes. Their most important features are (Resman et al., 2021):

- Flexibility and efficient production. Rebuilding a production line and adjusting the mode of operation of industrial machinery is in any case a major financial and organizational challenge. It requires complex decisions backed by meticulous analysis and research to avoid costly mistakes. Efficient adjustment of processes in Smart Factories is possible, among other things, thanks to the consistent use of tools such as digital twins. Such software allows virtual simulation and performance evaluation of new manufacturing processes before they are implemented. 3D printing, on the other hand, facilitates the rapid development of prototypes and product modifications before the final launch of industrial-scale production. In this way, technology makes it possible to diversify production tasks with limited risk.
- Application of intelligent robots. To ensure the adaptability of Smart Factories, in addition to the aforementioned digital technologies, appropriate automated systems are necessary. In smart manufacturing, industrial machines are transformed from ordinary devices with limited maneuvers into much more versatile systems capable of interacting with the environment. Examples of such solutions are the so-called cobots, or collaborative robots, as well as mobile robots. What's more, the control tools used in Smart Factories provide comprehensive supervision of production,

continuously collecting data from various types of sensors. The collected information is used to optimize processes – enabling, for example, the efficient use of available raw materials or reducing energy consumption by improving the efficiency of equipment operation.

- Greater process safety and efficiency. Industrial automation means less worker involvement, which in turn reduces the risk of personal injury and musculoskeletal trauma. In addition, machines are equipped with advanced sensors and safety protocols to further protect personnel.
- Smart Factories work with detailed preventive maintenance programs to reduce production downtime. This is one of the most promising developments in machine learning applications, as failures and defects reduce productivity and increase production time. Using data in decision-making processes, Smart Factories can efficiently extract data from the real world and use it in a digital environment. Integration with other highly specialized logistics systems (MES, ERP and especially WMS) provides a free flow of information that can be used for broader analysis. As a result, Smart Factories enable more complete process control, providing vital technical knowledge useful for strategic decision-making.

Smart Factories enable more complete control of processes, providing vital technical knowledge useful for strategic decision-making. Figure 3.1 shows the key elements of a Smart Factory.

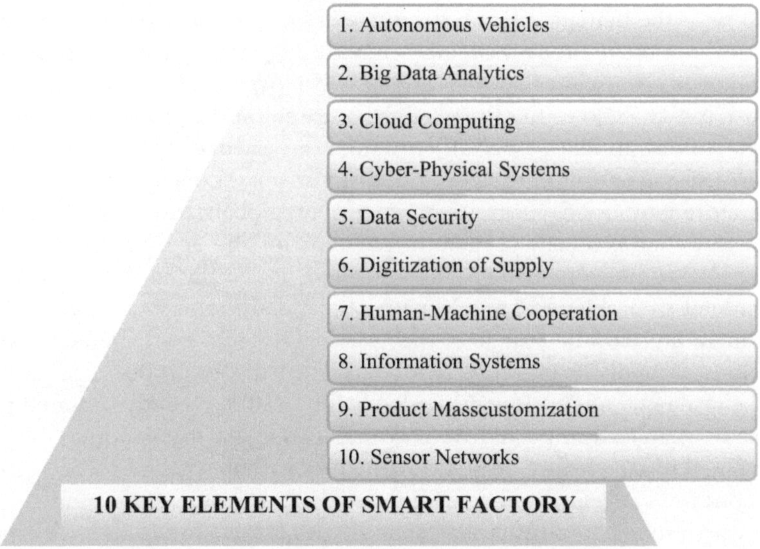

Figure 3.1 Key elements of the Smart Factory

Source: Authors' elaboration.

The Smart Factories at scale report published by the Capgemini Research Institute (2019) shows that companies are already applying smart manufacturing strategies to 30% of their processes and plan to extend them to another 40% of tasks in the coming years. As many as 68% of surveyed manufacturers say they have implemented smart manufacturing projects in their plants.

The data shows a clear, though still slow, upward trend. Smart Factories continue to face challenges, which in many cases represent a major obstacle to rapid development. For example, for 46% of those surveyed, cybersecurity is the biggest problem and for 51%, the lack of technical integration capabilities (most often due to a shortage of specialists with skills to match Worker 4.0).

Network forms of cooperation between small and medium enterprises

The dynamic growth of competition, largely related to the globalization of the economy, makes it necessary to create a business concept that can meet the challenges of Industry 4.0. The Industry 4.0 concept is oriented toward high productivity of industrial systems and high profitability of implemented production projects. Noteworthy is the increase in the productivity of the resources used, the increase in production flexibility and the possibility of organizing the production of more personalized products. This means the ability to meet customer expectations without compromising the profitability of the production process of the offered product, thanks to the dynamic adjustment of autonomous modules of the entire process of preparation, production and delivery of the product to the customer. It combines the advantages of made-to-order production with the benefits of mass production today. Moreover, it is possible to significantly improve production efficiency through using material, production and employee resources of cooperating network partners with unused production capacity. This intensifies the need for research on the problems of developing new business models, especially oriented to network forms of cooperation of enterprises operating in the era of the Industry 4.0 concept.

The aforementioned progressive process of globalization, which initially seemed to be an excellent development factor for the economies of Western Europe, also turned out to be dangerous and, especially in recent years, has brought a lot of problems. The COVID-19 pandemic and various geopolitical issues, including conflicts such as the war in Ukraine, contributed to severe disruptions in supply chains. The lack of components for production, problems with the resilience of developed supply chains and the recently outlined problem of raw materials imported from countries subject to economic sanctions (especially Russia) prompt reflection on the current strategy for developing local economies and small- and medium-sized enterprises.

The use of modern Industry 4.0 technologies, adaptation of the servitization strategy and narrow specialization of enterprises are significant. Industry 4.0 is an excellent tool to activate local economies and the SME sector and quickly become independent from uncertain markets characterized by low labor costs. Another advantage of developing local small- and medium-sized enterprises is the drastic increase in logistic expenses caused by high crude oil prices. This can be seen as an opportunity to intensify the development of local enterprises, which can take over the activities carried out in extensive supply chains on local markets.

Nowadays, every company should be seen as an intelligent module that can be used in the network. The size of the enterprise is, therefore, no longer relevant. What is essential, however, is the level of technology used, the level of highly qualified staff employed and the openness to unlimited communication and networking, that is, cooperation in the network.

In general, Industry 4.0 is to create sophisticated networks of enterprises connected by intelligent resources communicating via the Internet. This is a challenge for modern enterprises, especially small and medium ones, which must cooperate within the framework of cyber-physical systems to survive in the market.

W. Czakon defined networks of enterprises as "a specific space for cooperation between relatively independent entities, created for their common or individual goals, in which there are economic and social ties, and management is carried out through contracts and interpersonal decision-making processes" (Czakon, 2005). The essence of any enterprise network, including the production network, is the cooperation of partners, which leads to the achievement of the synergy effect, the effect of which is achieved by using the available potential (know-how, technological resources, means of communication, technology, etc.) to achieve a common goal of the entire network. The crucial role of the network coordinator (network broker, network leader), who acts as the organizer of the transfer of tangible and intangible assets in the network structure and who is responsible for the efficiency of this coordination to achieve the network synergy effect, is pointed out by S. Lachiewicz and A. Zakrzewska-Bielawska (2012). In classic networks, the coordinator's task is to identify business opportunities and organize the enterprise network. This is often a significant problem, especially in selecting network partners and responsibility for joint ventures or settlements between partners. Unfortunately, in practice, there is still a lack of appropriate procedures and tools, including IT tools, supporting establishing and managing such a network organization. Industry 4.0 created new, more favorable conditions for the cooperation of resources and, above all, the ability to transfer essential data about resources and progress on implementing individual operations in real time between resources and network partners.

Thanks to new business models of cooperating enterprises and Industry 4.0 technologies enabling communication of intelligent resources, modern enterprise networks can offer more complex, innovative products and services tailored to customers' needs, combining their potential into a network organization (Walters & Buchanan, 2001). Nowadays, companies must completely change their strategy, create new business models and overcome many operational and technological barriers. The most significant obstacles are in the following four areas (Figure 3.2):

- Technical infrastructure – the use of intelligent machines and devices, autonomous transport, digital monitoring devices, and so on;
- Automation of machines and devices operation and communication;
- Industry 4.0 technologies, big data, Industrial Internet of Things, cloud computing, augmented reality and so on;
- Cooperation with other companies – building relationships and developing competencies that will allow cooperation in the creation of cyber-physical networks of enterprises;
- Employee competencies – employee skills needed to implement the Industry 4.0 concept, supervise and develop digital technologies and manage cyber-physical enterprise systems
- Business models of cooperating small and medium enterprises.

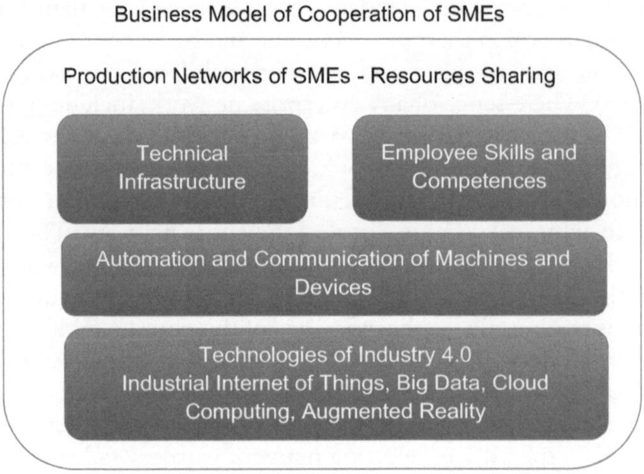

Figure 3.2 Key areas of barriers to networking small- and medium-sized enterprises in the Industry 4.0 environment

Source: Authors' elaboration.

In each of the aforementioned areas, it is possible to identify strategic goals that must be achieved to successfully implement the assumptions of the Industry 4.0 concept. The condition for developing enterprise networking in the states of Industry 4.0 is developing a business model of cooperation between enterprises operating within cyber-physical networks. The idea of a cyber-physical production network means the production of joint production orders using fully automated processes of individual network partners. Communication occurs via the Internet, and the necessary data is stored in the cloud (cloud technology). It enables constant access of all network participants to selected, essential information from anywhere in the world. Modern communication systems should primarily ensure automatic data collection, processing and impact on physical processes occurring throughout the entire production network thanks to unlimited network connections of intelligent, mechatronic resources that communicate with each other (machines, devices, robots, means of transport, etc.). Thus, the opportunity for development appears in creating a partnership combining specialized competencies and the ability to change to meet customer expectations better and effectively gain a competitive advantage in the market (Grabowska & Saniuk, 2021).

Today's small and medium enterprises are more open to communication and cooperation. New technologies favor the exchange of information in Big Data in real time and the automation of business processes related to the implementation of joint production projects. Networking is additionally forced by the need for a narrow specialization of enterprises that change their product-oriented strategy into a strategy based on the services of manufacturing systems. Servitization promotes the development of network cooperation between enterprises and allows for better customer orientation (Grabowska & Saniuk, 2022). Unfortunately, the level of their adjustment significantly differs from the requirements imposed by the Industry 4.0 concept. They are performing the role of an integrated, intelligent module that sends and receives information streams via ICT networks and performs tasks within the supply chain. It requires significant investments in terms of the technologies used and the level of education of employees and management staff (Saniuk et al., 2021). One of the considerable problems of enterprise networking is the selection of network partners, where several features describing the network partner should be taken into account, for example, its production capabilities, technology, the quality level of services offered, financial condition, experience, communication skills, and so on (Franke, 2001). Each of these areas significantly impacts the results of joint implementation of tasks. An equally important problem is trust in partners, the need to invest in information technology and issues with its use. This mainly affects small and medium enterprises, which make limited use of advanced IT technologies due to high implementation and service costs.

Building a network model, therefore, requires the development of a set of conditions related to the way the enterprise operates in the production network, establishing temporary networks oriented to a joint production venture, planning the load of geographically dispersed resources, production control or financial settlement of partners providing resources for production.

Entering an enterprise with such a model of a cyber-physical network operating under the Industry 4.0 concept requires a preliminary assessment of the company's technological potential, know-how, employee competencies and ability to cooperate by sharing resources. Important from the point of view of enterprises' adaptation to the implementation of the Industry 4.0 concept is (based on Soszyńska, 2012, p. 198):

- reducing the technological gap in the field of automation and digitization as well as digital technologies identified with Industry 4.0;
- digitization of products and services;
- enhancing the socio-technological potential;
- strengthening the internal capacity to absorb and adapt innovation;
- focus on the individual needs of customers in the field of personalization of products and services;
- focus on network cooperation.

Considering the limited investment opportunities of small and medium enterprises, selecting an area/specialization in the network is essential. A narrow field allows you to focus on developing resources that guarantee a high level of use and will ensure the enterprise's competitiveness. Therefore, each enterprise should decide to what extent it will offer its services for network cooperation to limit the very high costs of technical infrastructure. Adopting strategic goals focused on implementing technology requires a stage related to identifying needs and determining the required resources and technologies capable of cooperation within the cyber-physical network. The last step is investing in the required resources and joining a common platform responsible for accepting orders from the client and organizing temporary networks of companies that provide mechatronic resources for the platform. A general diagram of the integration of network-oriented enterprises within the Industry 4.0 concept is shown in Figure 3.3.

An excellent opportunity to dynamize business models and cooperation of enterprises within the framework of the Industry 4.0 concept is the creation of enterprise networking platforms, that is, various types of platforms bringing together enterprises and organizing network forms of cooperation oriented to customer needs.

So far, the platforms in practice have acted as resource search engines that allow you to find a partner with spare production capacity quickly. An example is the Cluster of Innovative Technologies in Manufacturing CINNOMATECH, which offers a platform service for exchanging production capacities on its websites. The platform allows increasing the use of its resources and, if necessary, carrying out work on workstations in partner production plants. The proposed application lets you quickly find partners who offer spare production capacity in a specific category. The search can be general and done by typing the name of the machine/equipment or more specific by specifying additional parameters (CINNOMATECH, 2022).

A cluster associating enterprises is a perfect environment for organizing platforms due to the elimination of the problem of distrust toward partners. Cluster companies are pre-verified. The participation of especially small- and medium-sized enterprises in the cluster also brings benefits consistent with network cooperation and, thanks to the collaboration with local governments, research units and business environment institutions. It allows development in the field of research and development. The role of clusters in developing network forms of cooperation is invaluable. These are the organizations with the most significant potential for networking growth in the Industry 4.0 concept era. This is mainly due to the possibility of jointly applying for grants, better access to consulting and training services and better access to scientific units and university technology parks that can support research and development activities and transfer knowledge to industry.

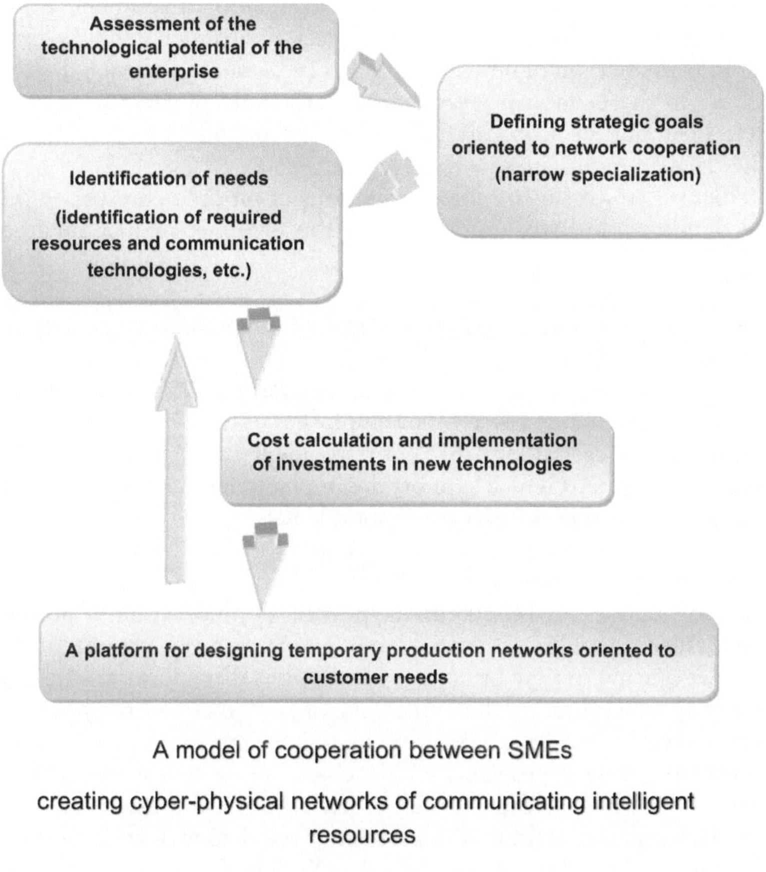

Figure 3.3 Model of integration of small and medium enterprises oriented to cooperation in the Industry 4.0 environment

Source: Authors' elaboration.

Unfortunately, despite the apparent benefits resulting from cooperation, there are still many concerns among small- and medium-sized enterprises related to creating various forms of collaboration.

The authors surveyed a selected group of 50 enterprises from the SME sector related to industrial production. The selection of the research sample was deliberate. Only enterprises interested in implementing the Industry 4.0 concept were examined. The study was conducted using the CAWI (Computer-Assisted Web Interview) method. The study shows that companies know the idea of Industry 4.0 and declare the implementation of Industry 4.0 technology in the future while admitting that they do not have a strictly developed implementation plan (92% of respondents).

The concerns identified during the survey include the low level of cybersecurity (79% of respondents) and high investment costs related to implementing Industry 4.0 technology (78% of respondents). Respondents also highlighted concerns about the low expected return on investment (over 75% of respondents). A significant problem is the lack of qualified staff who can support the implementation of new technologies (67% of respondents). Regarding networking in the economy, entrepreneurs are afraid of disloyal cooperation partners and emphasize problems finding an appropriate, reliable network partner. The detailed results are shown in Figure 3.4.

Particularly noteworthy are the expectations of modern enterprises, which, in their opinion, can significantly support the SME sector in implementing Industry 4.0 technology. These are:

- professional e-business platforms facilitating networking of enterprises (80% of respondents);
- business models describing network collaboration (72% of respondents);
- support for the training system for employees of the SME sector in the use of Industry 4.0 technology (67% of respondents);
- European programs which support the implementation of intelligent technologies of Industry 4.0 (55% of respondents).

One of the severe problems in small- and medium-manufacturing enterprises is the lack of support for IT systems supporting the estimation of production capacities, especially online. Networking of enterprises requires potential partners to react quickly to new business opportunities that appear on the market. The ability to quickly assess the availability of resources and the cost of their use by all network partners is a priority when building a production network.

Unfortunately, several problems and development barriers in the SME sector collide with the chances of quick implementation of the Industry 4.0 concept by the SME sector. In addition, the problem is the shallow level of automation and computerization of these enterprises, including the use of IT systems for operational management and control of production MES – (Manufacturing Execution System).

Other problems faced by small and medium enterprises include (Saniuk & Grabowska, 2021):

- no climate for investments in intelligent technologies (enterprises still prefer the role of marketing over modern technologies in building a competitive advantage in the market);

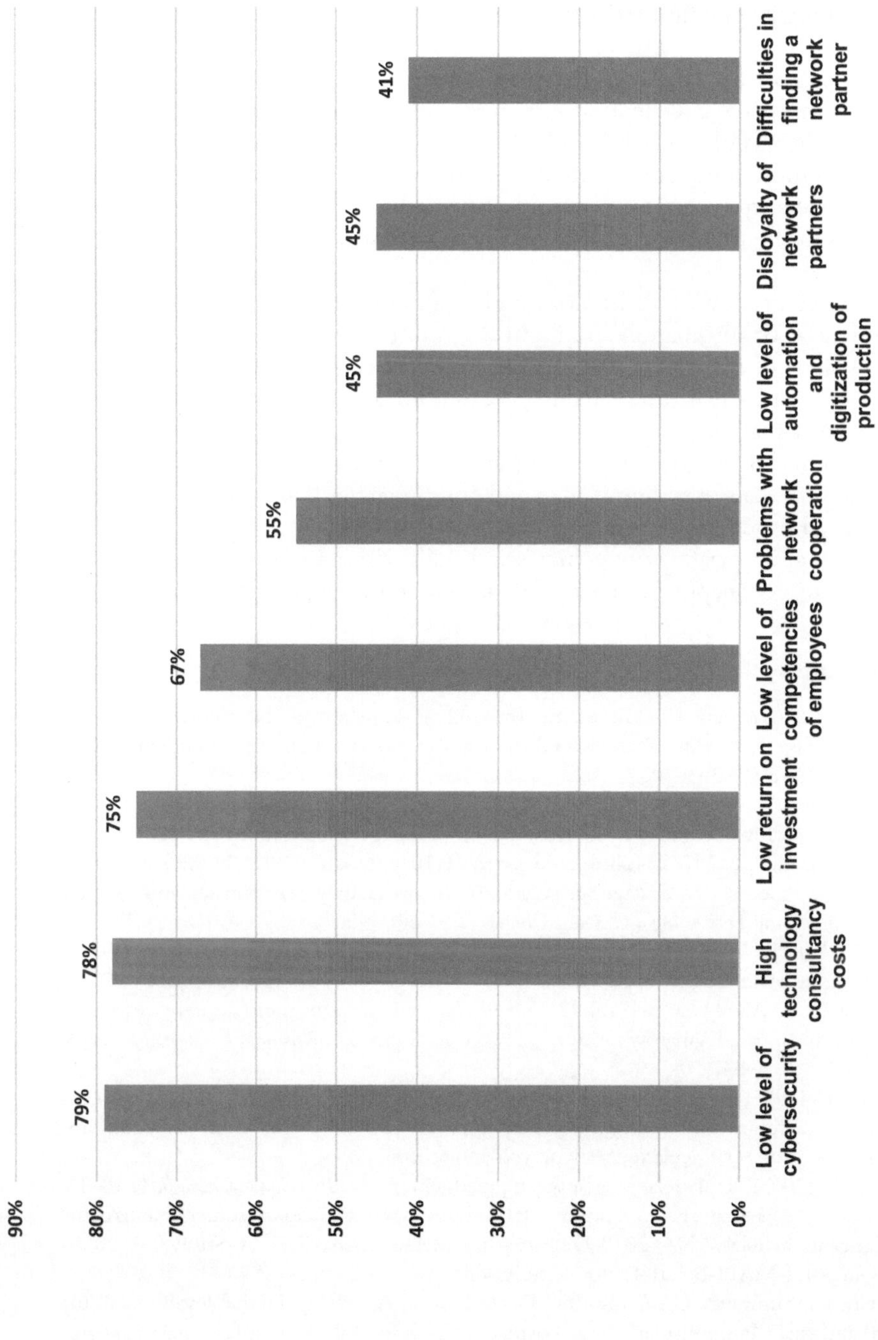

Figure 3.4 Main barriers of Industry 4.0 implementation and network cooperation of SMEs

Source: Authors' elaboration.

- lack and low level of qualifications of the employed managerial and engineering staff, especially in the field of computerization and digitization;
- low wages of employees, which discourage entrepreneurs from investing in changing production techniques from labor-intensive to capital-intensive.

Industry 4.0 is a big challenge for small- and medium-sized enterprises, but at the same time it has excellent development prospects in the future. To function in the conditions of the fourth industrial revolution, small- and medium-sized enterprises must completely change their strategy and overcome many barriers. As can be seen from the observations presented, the most significant obstacles are found in the following areas (Saniuk & Grabowska, 2021):

- insufficient modern technology and IT infrastructure;
- low level of automation and digitization of processes;
- low level of use of Big Data technology (collection, exchange and analysis of data in real time, enabling communication of resources and quick decision-making);
- problems related to network cooperation of enterprises (building relationships and transfer of knowledge and competencies thanks to jointly implemented production projects);
- lack of appropriate competencies and skills of employees needed to implement the concept of Industry 4.0 and network cooperation.

Bibliography

Aubin, C. A., Gorissen, B., Milana, E., Buskohl, P. R., Lazarus, N., Slipher, G. A., & Shepherd, R. F. (2022). Towards enduring autonomous robots via embodied energy. *Nature*, *602*(7897), 393–402.

Bandyopadhyay, A., Traxel, K. D., Lang, M., Juhasz, M., Eliaz, N., & Bose, S. (2022). Alloy design via additive manufacturing: Advantages, challenges, applications and perspectives. *Materials Today*, *52*, 207–224. https://doi.org/10.1016/j.mattod.2021.11.026

Büchi, G., Cugno, M., & Castagnoli, R. (2020). Smart factory performance and industry 4.0. *Technological Forecasting and Social Change*, *150*, 119790.

Chen, B., Wan, J., Shu, L., Li, P., Mukherjee, M., & Yin, B. (2017). Smart factory of industry 4.0: Key technologies, application case, and challenges. *IEEE Access*, *6*, 6505–6519.

Chrzanowski, A. A., & Glażewska, I. (2016). Wpływ rewolucji technologicznej na ewolucję strategicznych paradygmatów zarządzania przedsiębiorstwem. *Kwartalnik Naukowy Uczelni Vistula*, *2*(48), 5–34.

CINNOMATECH – Klaster Innowacyjnych Technologii w Wytwarzaniu, Platforma Wymiany Zdolności Produkcyjnych. Retrieved August 18, 2022, from www.cinnomatech.pl/pl/strony/1059.platforma-wolnych-mocy.html

Czakon, W. (2005). Istota relacji sieciowych przedsiębiorstwa. *Przegląd organizacji*, *9*, 10–13.

Deloite and MAPI Smart Factory Study. (2019). https://www2.deloitte.com/content/dam/insights/us/articles/6276_2019-Deloitte-and-MAPI-Smart-Factory-Study/DI_2019-Deloitte-and-MAPI-Smart-Factory-Study.pdf

Donnelly, C., Simmons, G., Armstrong, G., & Fearne, A. (2015). Digital loyalty card 'big data' and small business marketing: Formal versus informal or complementary? *International Small Business Journal*, *33*(4), 422–442.

Erboz, G. (2017). How to define industry 4.0: Main pillars of industry 4.0. *Managerial Trends in the Development of Enterprises in Globalization Era, 761*, 767.

Evjemo, L. D., Gjerstad, T., Grøtli, E. I., & Sziebig, G. (2020). Trends in smart manufacturing: Role of humans and industrial robots in smart factories. *Current Robotics Reports, 1*(2), 35–41.

Franke, U. (2001). The concept of virtual web organizations and its implications on changing market conditions. *Electronic Journal of Organizational Virtualness, 3*.

Gabriel, M., & Pessl, E. (2016). Industry 4.0 and sustainability impacts: Critical discussion of sustainability aspects with a special focus on future of work and ecological consequences. *Annals of the Faculty of Engineering Hunedoara, 14*(2), 131.

Gajdzik, B., & Grabowska, S. (2018). Leksykon pojęć stosowanych w przemyśle 4.0. *Zeszyty Naukowe. Organizacja i Zarządzanie/Politechnika Śląska, 132*, 221–238. https://doi.org/10.29119/1641-3466.2018.132.14

García-Muiña, F. E., Medina-Salgado, M. S., Ferrari, A. M., & Cucchi, M. (2020). Sustainability transition in industry 4.0 and smart manufacturing with the triple-layered business model canvas. *Sustainability, 12*(6), 2364.

Ghobakhloo, M. (2020). Industry 4.0, digitization, and opportunities for sustainability. *Journal of Cleaner Production, 252*, 119869.

Ghondaghsaz, N., & Engesser, S. (2021). Identification of factors and outcomes of trust in mobile supply chains. *European Journal of Management and Business Economics, 31*, 325–344. https://doi.org/10.1108/ejmbe-05-2021-0155

Grabowska, S. (2020). Smart factories in the age of industry 4.0. *Management Systems in Production Engineering, 28*(2), 90–96. https://doi.org/10.2478/mspe-2020-0014

Grabowska, S., & Saniuk, S. (2021). Modern marketing for customized products under conditions of fourth industrial revolution. In J. Duda & A. Gąsior (Eds.), *Industry 4.0: A global perspective* (pp. 159–171). Taylor & Francis Group. https://doi.org/10.4324/9781003186373

Grabowska, S., & Saniuk, S. (2022a). Development of business models in the fourth industrial revolution: Conditions in the context of empirical research on worldwide scope companies located in Poland. *Journal of Open Innovation: Technology, Market, and Complexity, 8*(2), 1–20. http://doi.org/10.3390/joitmc8020086

Grabowska, S., & Saniuk, S. (2022b). Servitization and the business model of cyber-physical networks in the context of personalized production. *European Research Studies Journal, XXV*(1), 955–966.

Haleem, A., Javaid, M., Singh, R. P., Rab, S., & Suman, R. (2022). Perspectives of cybersecurity for ameliorative industry 4.0 era: A review-based framework. *Industrial Robot: The International Journal of Robotics Research and Application, 49*, 582–597. https://doi.org/10.1108/ir-10-2021-0243

Hermann, M., Pentek, T., & Otto, B. (2015). Design principles for industrie 4.0 scenarios: A literature review. *Technische Universität Dortmund, Dortmund, 45*.

Imam, N., Rao, N. S., Al-Najjar, A., Naughton, T., & Hitefield, S. (2022, April). Emulation framework for distributed large-scale systems integration. In *2022 IEEE international systems conference (SysCon)* (pp. 1–8). IEEE.

Imran, M., Hameed, W. U., & Haque, A. U. (2018). Influence of industry 4.0 on the production and service sectors in Pakistan: Evidence from textile and logistics industries. *Social Sciences*, 7(12), 246.

Industry 4.0 How to navigate digitization of the manufacturing sector. (2015). www.mckinsey.com/~/media/McKinsey/Business%20Functions/Operations/Our%20Insights/Industry%2040%20How%20to%20navigate%20digitization%20of%20the%20manufacturing%20sector/Industry-40-How-to-navigate-digitization-of-the-manufacturing-sector.ashx

Janik, A., & Ryszko, A. (2018, November). Mapping the field of industry 4.0 based on bibliometric analysis. *International Business Information Management Association Conference (IBIMA), 32*.

Javadpour, A., Abadi, A. M. H., Rezaei, S., Zomorodian, M., & Rostami, A. S. (2022). Improving load balancing for data-duplication in big data cloud computing networks. *Cluster Computing, 25*(4), 2613–2631.

Lachiewicz, S., & Zakrzewska-Bielawska, A. (2012). Sieć przedsiębiorstw jako skuteczna forma organizacyjna w warunkach kryzysu gospodarczego. *Management and Business Administration. Central Europe, 20*(4), 34–45.

Lasi, H., Fettke, P., Kemper, H. G., Feld, T., & Hoffmann, M. (2014). Industry 4.0. *Business & Information Systems Engineering, 6*(4), 239–242.

Lee, R. L. (2022). When masses re-individualize: Affect, contagion and control in digital modernity. *Distinktion: Journal of Social Theory*, 1–15.

Lehmann, M. A., Porsch, R., & Mai, C. (2021). Assembly process digitization through self-learning assistance systems in production. In *Towards sustainable customization: Bridging smart products and manufacturing systems* (pp. 216–223). Springer.

Longo, F., Nicoletti, L., & Padovano, A. (2017). Smart operators in industry 4.0: A human-centered approach to enhance operators' capabilities and competencies within the new smart factory context. *Computers & Industrial Engineering, 113*, 144–159.

Mabkhot, M. M., Al-Ahmari, A. M., Salah, B., & Alkhalefah, H. (2018). Requirements of the smart factory system: A survey and perspective. *Machines, 6*(2), 23.

Machado, C. G., Winroth, M. P., & Ribeiro da Silva, E. H. D. (2020). Sustainable manufacturing in Industry 4.0: An emerging research agenda. *International Journal of Production Research, 58*(5), 1462–1484.

Maresova, P., Soukal, I., Svobodova, L., Hedvicakova, M., Javanmardi, E., Selamat, A., & Krejcar, O. (2018). Consequences of industry 4.0 in business and economics. *Economies, 6*(3), 46.

Müller, J. M., Kiel, D., & Voigt, K. I. (2018). What drives the implementation of industry 4.0? The role of opportunities and challenges in the context of sustainability. *Sustainability, 10*(1), 247.

Naeem, M., Jamal, T., Diaz-Martinez, J., Butt, S. A., Montesano, N., Tariq, M. I., & De-La-Hoz-Valdiris, E. (2022). Trends and future perspective challenges in big data. In *Advances in intelligent data analysis and applications* (pp. 309–325). Springer.

Olsen, T. L., & Tomlin, B. (2020). Industry 4.0: Opportunities and challenges for operations management. *Manufacturing & Service Operations Management, 22*(1), 113–122.

Paula Ferreira, W. D., Palaniappan, A., Armellini, F., Santa-Eulalia, L. A. D., Mosconi, E., & Marion, G. (2021). Linking industry 4.0, learning factory and simulation: Testbeds and proof-of-concept experiments. In *Artificial intelligence in industry 4.0* (pp. 85–96). Springer.

Rauch, E., Matt, D. T., & Dallasega, P. (2015, March). Mobile on-site factories – Scalable and distributed manufacturing systems for the construction industry. In *2015 International conference on industrial engineering and operations management (IEOM)* (pp. 1–10). IEEE.

Resman, M., Turk, M., & Herakovič, N. (2021). Methodology for planning smart factory. *Procedia CIRP, 97*, 401–406.

Rojko, A. (2017). Industry 4.0 concept: Background and overview. *International Journal of Interactive Mobile Technologies, 11*(5).

Saniuk, S, Caganova, D., & Saniuk, A. (2021). Knowledge and skills of industrial employees and managerial staff for the industry 4.0 implementation. *Mobile Networks and Applications, 26*(2), 1–11.

Saniuk, S., & Grabowska, S. (2021). The concept of cyber-physical networks of small and medium enterprises under personalized manufacturing. *Energies, 14*(17), 5273. https://doi.org/10.3390/en14175273

Serror, M., Hack, S., Henze, M., Schuba, M., & Wehrle, K. (2020). Challenges and opportunities in securing the industrial internet of things. *IEEE Transactions on Industrial Informatics, 17*(5), 2985–2996.

Shi, Z., Xie, Y., Xue, W., Chen, Y., Fu, L., & Xu, X. (2020). Smart factory in industry 4.0. *Systems Research and Behavioral Science, 37*(4), 607–617.

Siegert, J., Schlegel, T., Zarco, L., Miljanovic, B., Meyke, A., & Bauernhansl, T. (2020). Ultra-flexible factories: An approach to manage complexity. *Procedia CIRP, 93*, 329–334.

Sjödin, D. R., Parida, V., Leksell, M., & Petrovic, A. (2018). Smart factory implementation and process innovation: A preliminary maturity model for leveraging digitalization in manufacturing moving to smart factories presents specific challenges that can be addressed through a structured approach focused on people, processes, and technologies. *Research-Technology Management, 61*(5), 22–31.

Smart factories. (2019). www.capgemini.com/wp-content/uploads/2019/11/Report-%E2%80%93-Smart-Factories.pdf

Soszyńska, E. (2012). Konwergencja technologiczna a potencjał społeczno-technologiczny krajów Unii Europejskiej. *Metody Ilościowe w Badaniach Ekonomicznych, XIII*(3), 191–201.

Stock, T., & Seliger, G. (2016). Opportunities of sustainable manufacturing in industry 4.0. *Procedia CIRP, 40*, 536–541.

Sudhoff, M., Leineweber, S., Linsinger, M., Niemeyer, J. F., & Kuhlenkötter, B. (2020). Objective data acquisition as the basis of digitization in manual assembly systems. *Procedia CIRP, 93*, 1176–1181.

Thoben, K. D., Wiesner, S., & Wuest, T. (2017). "Industrie 4.0" and smart manufacturing-a review of research issues and application examples. *International Journal of Automation Technology, 11*(1), 4–16.

Walters, D., & Buchanan, J. (2001). The new economy, new opportunities and new structures. *Management Decision, 39*(10), 822–823.

Weking, J., Stöcker, M., Kowalkiewicz, M., Böhm, M., & Krcmar, H. (2020). Leveraging industry 4.0–A business model pattern framework. *International Journal of Production Economics, 225*, 107588.

Xiong, J., Hsiang, E. L., He, Z., Zhan, T., & Wu, S. T. (2021). Augmented reality and virtual reality displays: Emerging technologies and future perspectives. *Light: Science & Applications, 10*(1), 1–30.

Yılmaz, Ö. (2021). Loneliness of the precariat and psychopolitics. *Academia Letters, 2*. www.academia.edu/49879392/Loneliness_of_the_Precariat_and_Psychopolitics

4 A concept for planning cyber-physical production networks

Customer and manufacturer integration platform model

The need to offer highly personalized products on the market forces companies to change the current "modus operandi" to increase the interaction between the producer and the consumer. Nowadays, consumers want to participate (have an impact) in the process of designing, manufacturing and determining the method of delivering a product to the customer. They expect products tailored to their personal needs, preferences, tastes and lifestyle. They want to influence the configuration of the manufactured products and, simultaneously, require a price similar to the products offered in series production. Today's consumer of personalized products is treated as a customer of a manufacturing enterprise, not an anonymous consumer of products in the shopping center. This means tightening the interaction between the customer and the manufacturer. Manufacturers are increasingly using World Class Manufacturing (WCM) standards, production to order, rational resource management, development of network forms of cooperation, automation and robotization of production, transfer of some processes to customers, for example, co-design, assembly, product improvement and so on (Niehoff & Beier, 2018). A significant improvement in production efficiency is achieved thanks to personalization and strategy "make to order," which directly leads to savings in material, energy, production resources and an increase in work efficiency (Blom & Monk, 2003). The resources used account for the largest share of the overall production costs, ultimately affecting the possibility of reducing the product's price. The direction of changes in the pursuit of saving resources is consistent with the general principles of sustainable development. Products made following the "zero waste" principle are sustainable products. Also, it should be emphasized that the client's growing awareness of the need to protect the environment and reduce pollution caused by excessive production of goods and services. This is mainly related to implementing the sustainable production and consumption strategy discussed in more detail in Chapter 1.

Generally, personalized products and services and efficiently implemented marketing communication increase customer loyalty. Developing a scheme to ensure communication with the customer during the personalization of the

DOI: 10.4324/9781003317401-5

purchased product results in mass personalization (Senanayake & Little, 2010). Mass personalization requires that the product be adaptable and configurable because not only the final product but also the design and packaging process should allow for product differentiation according to individual preferences (Stock & Seliger, 2016). Today, a wide range of products are personalized. Personalization of products is made of commonly available shoes where the customer measures the foot electronically, selects colors, laces, personalized inscriptions and even designs the shoe's shape in specially prepared electronic customer service points of such companies as Adidas, Nike, Timberland and Converse or Burberry. The equipment of expensive luxury cars, such as Maybach or Ferrari, is also subject to personalization. In any case, it requires the manufacturer to incur significant expenses related to creating an interface for communication with the customer and cooperation with numerous suppliers who can quickly and flexibly adapt to the customer's needs. Specialized software is also an excellent tool for researching consumer preferences and expectations as to the innovative features of a newly designed product.

The necessity to offer personalized products requires constant monitoring of customer expectations. An example is using such an application by the Fiat concern when designing the Fiat 500 model. Fiat has received over 160,000 configuration proposals from potential customers. Potential customers expressed expectations regarding the car's equipment even before the start of the series production of this model. Another way to integrate the customer with the manufacturer is to match the manufactured assortment to the needs of a specific customer. Such a solution was introduced by eobuwie.pl and CCC, which use the esize.me service of scanning the customer's foot and available products. Specialized software selects the needed footwear to the individual size of the client's foot. Similarly, the range is adapted by the clothing manufacturer Zafu, which indicates products tailored to a specific type of customer's figure on its website. From the producer's point of view, these are standard products that provide their customers with personalized values. Nowadays, many cosmetic companies offer personalization services. For example, the German brand Schwarzkopf (Henkel) is preparing to test its "salon-lab" design in hair salons in Western Europe and Japan. They will offer a service of personalized shampoos adapted to the consumer's hair.

The Fourth Industrial Revolution is changing B2B (Business to Business) and B2C (Business to Customer) relationships, eliminating traditional competitive strategies and favoring the emergence of more and more complex business models that require innovative marketing activities and intensification of interaction with customers (Berger, 2016). The change also applies to producing and delivering products to the market. There is a definite shift from the push model to the pull model, in which end recipients decide what products they want to receive. This means that the need to understand the individual preferences of users (and thus the creation of their psychographic profiles) helps in the selection of specific products or brands and, to a large extent, in communication methods (Dunn, 2015). Having information about the client and knowledge of their interests and habits allows them to adjust the offer to their individual needs better.

The most important feature of the customer–producer (manufacturer) interaction in the last decade is the dynamic penetration of mobile devices and the collection of customer data from various sources. Using applications on phones and active participation in social media blur the boundaries between the virtual and real world. Since mobile devices allow us to stay in constant contact with the Internet today, we generate more and more data that accurately describes our lives. This data is precious from a marketing point of view. This trend leads to a shift in the producer's interaction with the customer. The participation of a modern producer in Internet networks and advertising products and services on social networks is becoming a necessity today. New ways of interpersonal interactions that allow you to build relationships without geographic and demographic barriers in the virtual world translate into a way of building business relationships in the interactions between business partners and the client. Creating shared value with the customer must be based on digital marketing, that is, conducting advertising activities via the Internet in various commercial and social networks (Lies, 2017). To be successful in a global market, you need to be highly flexible and innovative and enter the online services market. A modern client is looking for information about the producer, product reviews on social media, asks questions on various websites and does not believe in traditional marketing messages offered only on the company's official websites (Maresova et al., 2018). A clear direction of changes in building the competitiveness of modern companies is the creation of value by customers. This means that customers take actions that affect the final composition of what they or other customers receive from the company – this can be considered a trend for Marketing 4.0.

As confirmed by the research results presented in work (Grabowska & Saniuk, 2021), we are currently dealing with customer-centricity. In the face of dynamic market changes, businesses cannot remain indifferent to the growing expectations of consumers. These expectations concern products, prices, promotions, added value or building relationships with the company. Consumers expect a personalized product because such a product makes them feel special. Most often, the respondents are willing to purchase personalized clothing and footwear, electronic equipment, catering services, personalized accessories and jewelry. Consumers are only willing to pay more for personalizing a product in exceptional cases; this means that it is necessary to develop the idea of Industry 4.0 to enable a high level of personalization at low production costs.

Based on the conducted research, consumers are characterized by different levels of expectations as to their involvement in the process of creating a personalized product. In the case of clothing, shoes, jewelry and food service, they expect pure personalization – they want to influence the design of new products. Home and garden equipment, automotive (cars) and electronics have slightly lower consumer expectations for a personalized effect. Pure standardization is expected in everyday products. For all product groups, consumers accept individual standardization that corresponds to current market trends. Thanks to the available data, predictive models and extensive personalization options, it is possible to reach the right customer with the right offer at the right time (Grabowska & Saniuk, 2021).

Digital technology introduces many changes in business models, management concepts, marketing instruments and the relationship between the producer and the customer. So in what direction will the activity of enterprises evolve today? Will the available data and technologies, such as the Internet of Things and AI, completely change the producer–customer relationship? These questions remain open-ended and require further research in this area.

Growing customer expectations are the main reason for developing the servitization of production systems and network forms of cooperation. Until now, mainly large enterprises could offer a high level of personalization. Nowadays, small and medium enterprises operating in the modern market are beginning to understand the need for changes, especially in implementing modern digital technologies and organizing intelligent cyber-physical networks of cooperating resources. New, more modern and innovative approaches to production and business management are associated with greater flexibility, efficiency and customer focus. The new production paradigm is changed in favor of the non-standard output, tailored to the needs of individual customers (Korena et al., 2015). The need to offer customers highly personalized products at low prices is forcing companies to change how they operate and focus on more interactions between the company and the customer. One of the ways to integrate small and medium-sized enterprises and their resources into the implementation of joint ventures oriented to the needs of a modern customer is to create a common customer–producer cooperation environment. Customer-driven businesses will likely fill the gap in a global, integrated supply chain for personalized manufacturing and services. Customers will design their products online through dedicated web-service platforms. An extremely flexible supply chain will produce "Batch Size 1" in real-time based on customer orders, leading to short lead times (Senanayake & Little, 2010).

By combining the potential of partners as a network organization, it will be possible to offer more complex, innovative products and services tailored to customers' needs (Saniuk et al., 2020). A practical approach to this approach is the organization of virtual business e-platforms. One of the critical tasks that they can perform in the customer–producer system is:

- establishing permanent or temporary relationships with the customer expecting an individualized product (order);
- co-creation (co-design) of a personalized product in close cooperation with the client by using the possibilities of graphical interfaces supporting the design of a new product;
- integration of resources of small- and medium-sized enterprises focused on cooperation with the platform and temporary or permanent sharing of their resources for the needs of network cooperation;

- planning and organization of cyber-physical networks dedicated to the implementation of specific personalized products (production orders).

The platform is, therefore, an interface between the customer and the product producer (temporary enterprise network). The customer can design and/or configure an individualized product online through the proposed offering of both products and production resource services. One of the concerns of using such an organization of production is product liability, which naturally results from the participation of several different economic actors involved in the production process. It is in the client's interest to build a liability model based on the liability of the seller of the product and not of individual network participants. Hence, the platform should constitute a separate economic entity that ensures the appropriate quality of the product and customer service.

Another problem is building a model of internal evaluation of the quality of services offered by network participants, verification of partners before starting the order and their evaluation after its completion. Also, it requires adopting the principles of responsibility for the entrusted tasks during the joint execution of orders. Another way is the naturally more and more commonly developed service insurance system for manufactured and sold goods, which will solve the problem of costs related to the replacement or repair of the product resulting from manufacturing defects.

Platforms are now available that support enterprises in the PaaS model – Platform-as-a-Service. Platforms of this type are consistent, secure and scalable tools supporting the creation of modern solutions for industry. They are a great tool, especially for small- and medium-sized enterprises that do not have to invest in additional IT infrastructure (servers, cybersecurity, data storage and so on). Enterprises pay only for services provided by the platform owner. An example of such services is the "Predix" platform, a modern IIoT platform developed by GE Digital. The platform provides users with a complete set of services, ranging from collecting data from machines with cybersecurity rules through process monitoring and data archiving in the cloud to Big Data analytics and advanced analytical applications, for example, Digital Twin (Predix – IIoT Platform, GE Digital, 2022).

An e-business platform should contain pre-verified companies with an appropriate level of quality of services, have know-how consistent with the requirements of potential customers, and proper material and logistics facilities. An essential criterion for cooperation is openness to implementing Industry 4.0 technologies, which enable the transfer of data about resources in real time, equipping production resources with appropriate devices (sensors) monitoring the status of order fulfillment in real time. At the same time, each company registered on the e-business platform has access only to information about emerging orders and can list the available resource as an offer for the resource service. Enterprises do not have access to the transferred data of other enterprise resources, especially regarding their availability or cost of use.

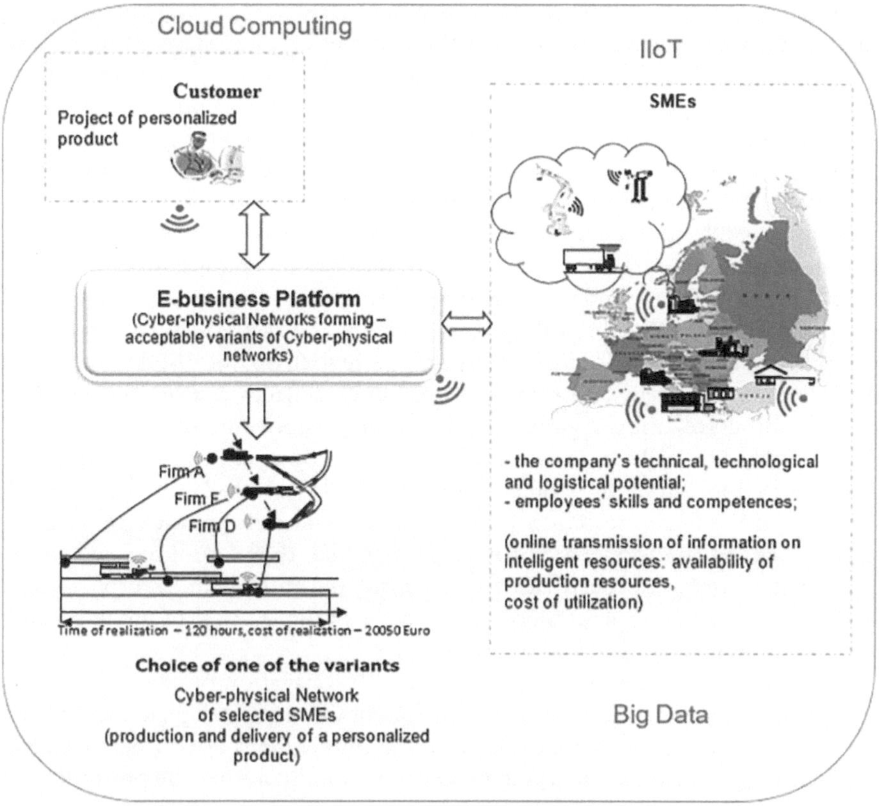

Figure 4.1 Model of the e-business platform of the customer-producer

Source: Authors' elaboration.

Data from enterprises should be automatically transferred to the platform from intelligent machines and devices in real time using advanced technologies, including Industrial Internet of Things, cloud computing and big data. The information exchange diagram and how the platform functions are shown in Figure 4.1 (Saniuk, 2022).

Concept of network prototyping methodology

The proposed solution is a kind of adaptive system, combining, on the one hand, the market requirements specified by production order, the implementation of which requires the involvement of specialized companies, and on the other hand, the production capabilities of geographically dispersed enterprises. As a result, temporary organizations (networks of enterprises) capable of adapting to the requirements of the planned production project are sought. Therefore, an answer to the question is sought: Is there a cyber-physical production network of enterprises capable of completing the order within a given time horizon and at the assumed costs? Searching for an answer to such a question requires checking the possibility of executing the order due to the available production capacities of enterprises and the possibility of carrying out transport operations between enterprises, with the assumed total cost of the order not exceeded. Based on the collected data and rapid prototyping algorithms, it becomes possible to generate a set of network variants that enable the timely execution of the order, taking into account production and logistics costs.

In practice, cyber-physical networks of enterprises are a combination of components of cyber-physical systems, which are composed of intelligent resources located in individual enterprises, essential for the production process. These components are resources (machines, devices, logistic means) that can communicate using appropriate data transmission infrastructure, such as the Internet (especially Internet of Things technology) and can work autonomously or cooperate with people remotely in real time. Today, cyber-physical networks of intelligent resources cover a vast spectrum of applications oriented to the needs of the modern customer. In practice, there are more and more cases of such organizations that can be considered intelligent enterprise networks, which dynamically undergo the process of digitization of processes and use a wide range of Industry 4.0 technologies.

The proposed methodology is based on the propagation of constraints, that is, checking sufficient conditions, the fulfillment of which will guarantee meeting the customer's expectations related to the timely delivery of a personalized product. In principle, the planning procedure should consider the possibility of rapid network prototyping, that is, the selection of companies that will meet the requirements related to the constraints of the order (time, price, quality and so on). At the same time, the planning methodology is required to provide a detailed network resource load plan (schedule) that will facilitate the process of controlling the production flow throughout the network. Until now, in systems of this type, the selection of resources was most often made in the form of bids in which the entrepreneur submitted bids to implement individual tasks. Currently, Industry 4.0 technologies such as Industrial Internet of Things, cloud computing and Big Data can be used for this purpose. Data on the current availability of intelligent enterprise resources can be transferred in real time to the platform and considered in generating new network variants in the event of the appearance of a new production order. Figure 4.2 shows the sequence of the phases of forming a cyber-physical network of enterprises.

Based on the proposed model of the e-business platform, the proposed concept of the methodology of forming a cyber-physical network can be presented as a three-phase procedure. In the first phase, the data of the production project is entered from the customer interface. The customer served by the platform in the electronic sales (e-commerce) system determines the need for a personalized product using the list of available product options or graphical product configuration interfaces. Based on the information collected from the client, appropriate construction and technological documentation for the personalized product is prepared with a detailed description of the technological process along with the separation of tasks and their technological consequences on all operations in the production order execution. After completing the production documentation and defining the cost and time frames of the order (negotiated with the client), the transaction broker responsible for contact with the client starts the second phase of network planning.

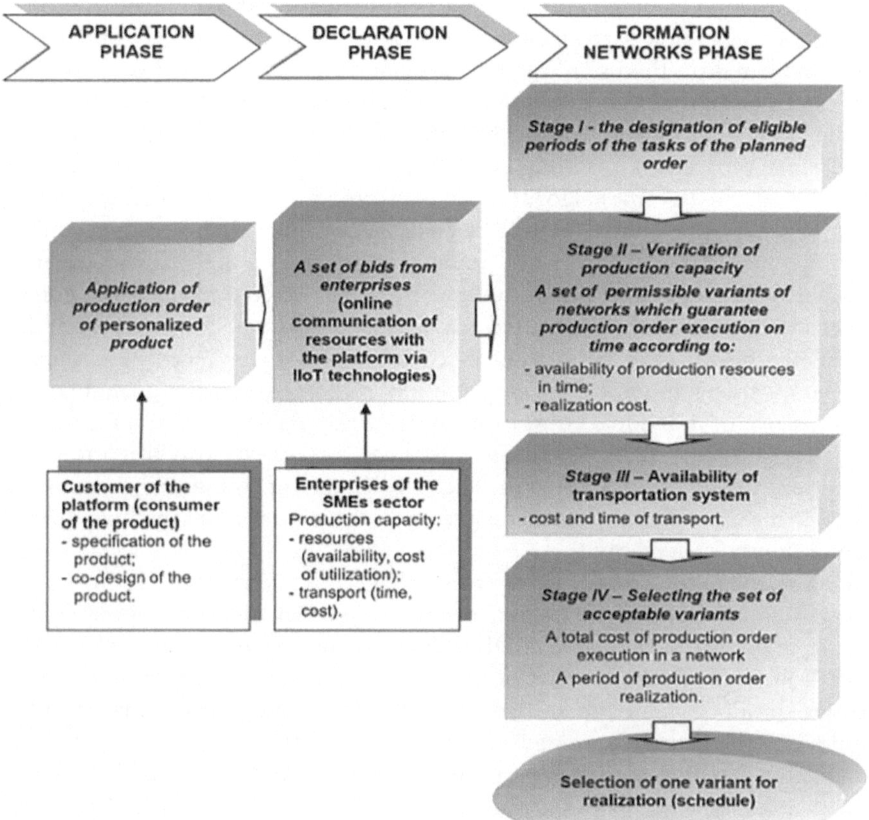

Figure 4.2 Methodology of cyber-physical networks of small and medium enterprises prototyping

Source: Authors' elaboration.

In the second phase, enterprises provide data on the availability of their resources. These data concern the type of resource, availability during the execution of the order, cost of use and efficiency. In this phase, offers are also collected from transport companies declaring the implementation of transport operations and logistic operators. With more technologically advanced resources, communication between the resource and the platform is automated, and it is possible to analyze the resource availability in real time.

In the last phase, the resources reported to the system are verified, and the permissible variants of production networks are prototyped. Based on the information collected in the platform system, the resources of enterprises will be selected, the availability of which guarantees the fastest possible execution of the order and shipment of the product to the customer. This stage is combined with developing a detailed load schedule for all partners making up the network. Due to the high combinatorial complexity of the problem of prototyping a cyber-physical production network in the third stage, an approach is proposed based on the use of rapid prototyping algorithms based on checking sufficient conditions, the fulfillment of which guarantees a proper execution of the order due to the existing resource, cost and logistic constraints. The third phase of network planning consists of four steps. The first stage uses the DFS (Depth First Search) algorithm to determine the date at which individual tasks of the planned order can be started and completed the earliest so that the implementation of the entire production process of the planned order is possible within a given time. In the next stage, the offered resources of enterprises are assigned to the designated task completion times. The number of the considered resources of enterprises (network variants) is reduced by eliminating those variants in which the availability of resources does not guarantee the performance of individual tasks. In stage III, the available set of resources (network variants) under consideration is limited to those variants that meet the conditions of the transport system. Each of the variants is assessed in terms of available means of transport and their capacity, which declares the implementation of transport operations.

Ultimately, in the considered approach, only those variants are distinguished that guarantee the implementation of the production order at the maximum cost assumed by the customer and the believed time horizon of the order. Each of the solutions obtained is a set of selected enterprises that can create a cyber-physical production network. Based on the determined total costs of order fulfillment, the dates of commencement and completion of tasks by established companies, one of the variants can be set, and the production can be carried out. Ultimately, for the chosen variant, a schedule burdening the resources of individual enterprises involved in implementing the joint venture is generated. Figure 4.3 shows an exemplary order fulfillment schedule for a selected company network. An example of a methodology for rapid prototyping of production networks using a prototype of a computer network planning system is presented, among others, at work (Saniuk & Saniuk, 2018).

The presented concept of enterprise network planning in the future should also be supported by the digital twin technology at the platform level, which will allow for efficient monitoring of resource work progress and implementation of manufacturing and logistics processes within the entire network in real

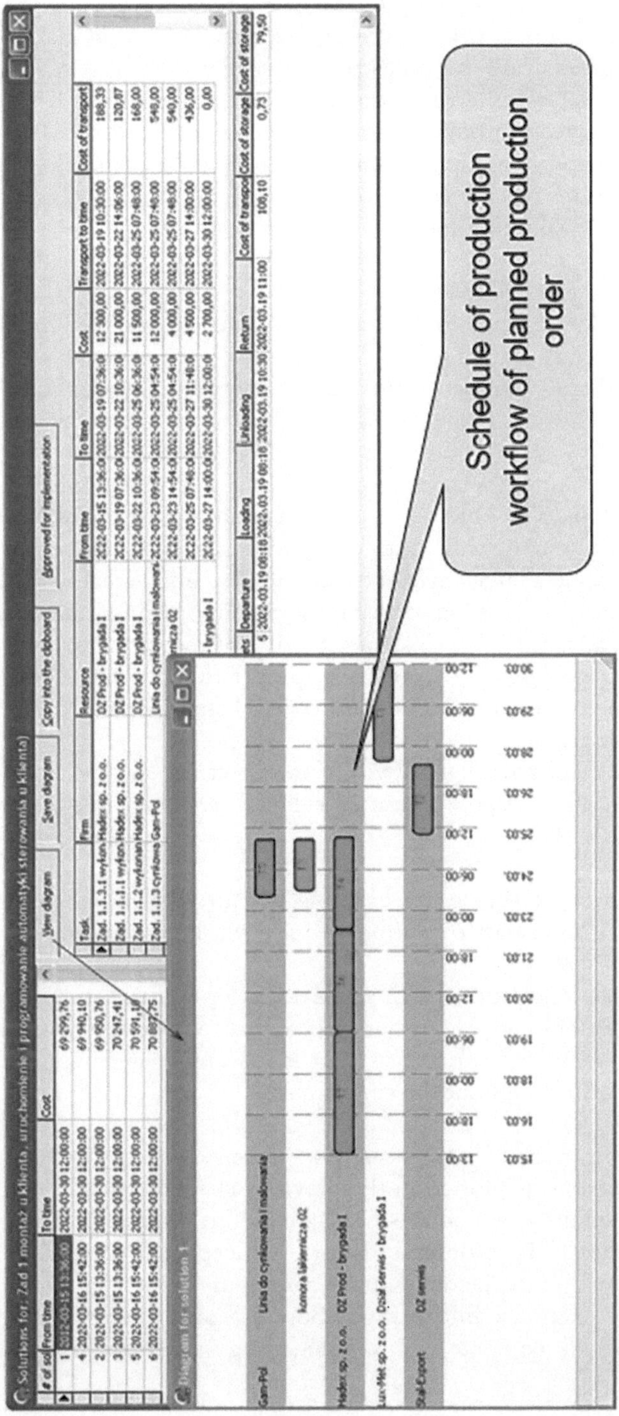

Figure 4.3 The choice of variant of the cyber-physical production network to realize the planned order with schedule

Source: Authors' elaboration.

time. A digital twin (DT) is a virtual model of a real enterprise, and in the case under consideration, a network of enterprises created based on real data from many sensors, sensors using the Industrial Internet of Things (IIoT) technology. Data is sent in real time to a computer, where algorithms based on AI analyze it and allow you to build a virtual image of reality. It is thanks to this that the digital version of a physical object can even better simulate the object and its behavior under specific conditions. The DT concept consists mainly of three elements (www.multiprojekt.pl, 2022):

- a physical object in real space;
- its digital model (scanned image or object simulator designed in the environment) placed in virtual space;
- an established real-time data connection between a physical and a digital object.

The technology is a kind of evolution of modeling and simulation methods or the "what if" analysis. The object is treated not as an ordinary 3D object but as a whole synergistic system. Simple statistical models cannot compete with the possibility of analyzing a huge amount of data flowing from a real object, which can be analyzed and visualized in virtual reality on an ongoing basis. Thanks to digital twins and advanced data analytics, the use of machine learning and AI algorithms, it is possible to find patterns of proper functioning of real objects and then implement "learning" a physical object based on the experiences of its digital counterpart.

The process of creating a digital twin of an object depends on the needs of a given company. The design and use of a digital twin can be considered on three levels (Rodak, 2021):

- a digital twin of a resource, for example, a critical machine that we want to improve or check its operation because we know or suppose it is a bottleneck;
- a digital twin of the process with all participating virtual machines;
- digital twin of business, that is, an approach in which we have digitized information about the entire business carried out by geographical enterprises dispersed throughout the supply chain.

The concept of organization of e-business platforms can be an excellent solution to many problems identified in the previous chapters related to adapting the small- and medium-sized enterprise sector to the conditions of the fourth industrial revolution. The proposed platform concept and network planning methodology provide intelligent resource communication, where enterprises can automatically exchange information about available resources in the network in real time and compete with capital-strong modern smart factories of the future.

The importance of collaboration and networking for the SME sector

The approach to cooperation within cyber-physical production networks presented in this chapter is a solution incredibly dedicated to specialized enterprises from the SME sector, which have minimal potential to create intelligent factories independently. One of the significant advantages is the possibility of creating modern alliances of enterprises based on the latest communication and data transfer technologies. Enterprises can focus their attention on the development of specialization, know-how and sales, not so much on products as services offered by their production systems. With the possibility of simultaneous involvement in many different projects (networks) within trusted e-business platforms, there is a potential possibility of obtaining a high level of resource use, which is especially important in times of economic crises.

A co-opetition strategy can be a successful strategy for high-tech enterprises. Instead of looking for a way to gain an advantage over market rivals, modern enterprises should concentrate their efforts on obtaining expected benefits (synergistic benefits) by maintaining mutual cooperative relations within the framework of a collaborative arrangement. One of the significant benefits of co-opetition is learning from your partner by sharing knowledge and information. The benefits include access to complementary resources, implying the expansion of the market offer, lowering the costs of the organization's operations, access to new technologies and production methods, development of competencies and so on. Also, co-opetition helps in acquiring new customers (Romaniuk, 2013). Based on the research by Zakrzewska-Bielawska on a representative sample of high-tech companies, it was found that co-opetition brings this type of enterprise more benefits than losses and contributes to their development and therefore is a source of their success (Zakrzewska-Bielawska, 2013).

Innovation is an essential feature of enterprises operating in networks. Numerous studies on cooperation between enterprises, including the creation of virtual relationships, confirm the thesis that cooperation between enterprises is conducive to the creation of innovation. The results of the Bosch-Sijtsema research from the case studies show that a high level of innovation occurs in organizations with a high level of virtualization (Bosch-Sijtsema). Travica argues that such intelligent organizations as cyber-physical networks manage knowledge perfectly. The ability to solve new problems in today's turbulent environment enables the sharing of knowledge and manifests itself in the use of knowledge. However, this ability may include other aspects such as improvisation, coincidence and wisdom (Travica, 2014).

The research problem of quick adaptation to the turbulent environment of the organization was solved by the model of dynamic abilities (Bogers et al., 2019). The dynamic capabilities of an organization are organizational and managerial processes of coordination/integration, learning and reconfiguration of resources. It is assumed that thanks to these processes, the company can integrate, build and reconfigure its competencies to meet customer expectations and changes in the environment. This approach assumes that external threats to the company's positioning are inevitable and permanent; therefore, the market should be constantly monitored, and attention should be paid to the process of reconfiguring the company's resources and developing organizational competencies. To interact with the client and to take advantage of crowdsourcing and networking, modern enterprises must implement systems of continuous monitoring of client needs, the use of new products, customer sentiment analysis, big data mining and their social media (Bogers et al., 2019; Travica, 2015).

Participation in the cyber-physical network of small- and medium-sized enterprises provides additional opportunities to access all kinds of missing resources (specialized equipment, technology, competencies, know-how, knowledge, etc.). Keeping the size of a small enterprise together with others as a cyber-physical network makes it possible to offer more complex, innovative products and services in the local, regional and even global markets (Walters & Buchanan, 2001). Since individual partners in the cyber-physical network are independent companies with a narrow specialization (specific competencies), orientation to a new product and exchange of knowledge between partners may occur faster than in large, often bureaucratic and inflexible enterprises.

Another positive feature of functioning in the network organization of a small- and medium-sized enterprise is the incurred operating costs. The enterprise network can incur high investment outlays with little (partial) involvement of individual participants. Each of the companies belonging to various alliances invests only in the area of its specialization, however, having the possibility of contracting all complementary functions with partners. The chance of occurring in many partnerships increases the productivity of the company's available production and human resources. Functioning in the network also positively influences the learning process through gaining experience, know-how and knowledge based on mutual relations between cooperating enterprises. The set of advantages from the cooperation of small- and medium-sized enterprises presented by Abreu and Camarinha-Matos (Abreu & Camarinha-Matos, 2008) perfectly coincides with the activities of enterprises in the cyber-physical network (see Table 4.1).

In practice, cyber-physical enterprise networks are a combination of components essential for production. These are resources (intelligent machines, devices, logistic means) that have communication capabilities using the appropriate data transmission infrastructure provided by the Internet of Things technology. Smart resources can work autonomously or collaborate with people remotely in real time. Today, cyber-physical networks of intelligent resources cover a vast spectrum of applications oriented to the needs of the modern customer and offer significant benefits for the development of the economy and society.

The benefits of network collaboration are evidenced by numerous cases of enterprises implementing Industry 4.0 technologies and collaborating within

Table 4.1 Aims of networking in the context of advantages of production network SMEs

Aims of networking	*Advantages and benefits for SMEs by networking*
Cost reduction and cost sharing	• SME have better access to new markets and/or businesses opportunities • Investment cost sharing, especially in ICT and Industry 4.0 technologies based on communication and data transfer • R&D costs sharing within cooperation with research centers and technology parks of universities • Co-financing of projects • Ability for SMEs to obtain lower prices for materials and raw materials
Sharing the risk	• Small and medium enterprises operate in turbulent environments and with limited, therefore imperfect, knowledge. Consequently, the level of uncertainty may hurt the decision-making processes. Sharing knowledge among partners allows a reduction of this uncertainty level • A partition of the responsibilities among partners (co-responsibility) • In the networks, solidarity mechanisms can be established among partners
Decreasing dependence level	• Companies depend on others to some extent for products, services, raw materials, tangible and intangible resources and competencies. Through cooperation, companies can reduce this dependence by creating privileged links to other firms in an attempt to reduce transaction costs that arise when uncertainty increases
Increasing innovation capacity	• Increasing the ability to generate new ideas by pooling existing resources and the diversity of cultures and experiences (critical mass) • The emergence of new sources of value • Shortening the life cycle of products and technologies • Possibility to develop more durable products that meet customer expectations and thus contribute to an increase in quality • Orientation on personalization of production and new products
Defend a strong position in the market	• Achievement of economies of scale by sharing resources • Establishment of defensive coalitions to build entry barriers to defend themselves against a dominant firm or a new player • Establishment of offensive coalitions to develop competitive advantages and strengthen their position by diminishing the other competitors' competitiveness • Increase the negotiation power in relation to suppliers and/or customers outside the collaborative network • The competition of SMEs with large companies
Flexibility increasing	• Share of resources and a combination of skills of partners • Using the core competencies from other partners • Increase the adaptation capacity toward several business environments simultaneously • The broader range of products/services on the market • Growth for new segments stably, reaching more considerable stability • Higher level of customization and customer orientation
Increasing agility	• Quickly respond to a business opportunity by establishing more flexible procedures • Increase the interoperability between several processes and products (establishment of norms)
Increasing specialization	• Focusing the company's activities on its resources and critical activities • Servitization strategy of SMEs • Customization

Source: Authors' elaboration based on Abreu and Camarinha-Matos (2008)

digital networks. An example of a Polish company for which the implementation of Industry 4.0 solutions was a strategic priority is a Polish manufacturer of gates, doors and fences (the company does not consent to the publication of the company's name). The company has invested in all value chain links to create a digital factory for mass production customization. The entire network of brand distributors has tools that enable the product's personalization for the end customer. Additionally, after placing an order, the IT system automatically generates technological parameters of production (including parameters of welding robots and control codes of mechanical processing machines). Thanks to this, it is possible to implement individualized production with negligible costs of retooling the system and thus reduction of unit costs of products. IT integration of the vertical value chain significantly reduces the delivery time of the final product, which translates into measurable business benefits. The applied robotic welding system increases production efficiency several times and optimizes the entire flow and order fulfillment process. The company is an excellent example of a modern approach to the customer who has the opportunity to participate in the design of personalized products and strengthen the relationship with the customer through the use of digital communication channels.

Another example of the digitization of processes and the creation of network connections between the customer and the manufacturer is a company operating in the international market that produces parts for the automotive sector. The company has created a platform for processing and visualizing production data. The company cooperates with numerous enterprises from the SME sector and uses the IIoT to process huge data sets in the cloud. The data collected by the company concerns all partners, production lines, individual machines and individual products and gives an insight into all performance indicators, allowing for real-time analysis and optimization of the value chain. The implementation of Industry 4.0 solutions began with defining the company's digital development strategy in 2013. Projects implemented in the company using the pillars of Industry 4.0 cover the entire value chain but to the greatest extent – production and logistics. Investments implemented in internal logistics include using RFID (radio frequency identification) technology that automatically registers the transported items and mediates the exchange of information between production and warehouse, using advanced Industry 4.0 solutions, such as automation and robotization of warehouse and transport activities. External logistics include exchanging information on products (cars) that have already left the factory. This enables product monitoring and software updates at the customer's site. Modules installed in vehicles have the latest available software version that controls them. The company is distinguished by a high degree of integration and automation in its production plants. Intelligent robots handle each stage of production. The use of the IIoT and the implementation of a network of wireless sensors in the enterprise to monitor the production and energy consumption of machines and technological installations enables the optimization of processes and the creation of performance benchmarks for other units of the company. Operators have mobile control tablets and virtual reality glasses; they constantly access all necessary data, enabling continuous monitoring. The factory management is centralized in one main building, which acts as the "central nervous system." Industry 4.0 solutions are used in individual plants of the enterprise to cover all aspects of the production process (materials, production systems, products, factory, energy management, safety technology and the evacuation process).

Digital twin is a concept that involves the creation of a virtual representation of enterprises, production systems or plant networks, the status of which is updated in real time. This allows you to monitor your environment and device health and perform simulations in virtual reality, saving time and money and making better decisions about future products and their new features. The development of digital twin technology can also facilitate building cyber-physical networks of enterprises. A consortium of Microsoft, Dell, Lendlease and Ansys (producer of software for simulation and spatial design) announced the creation of common standards and terminology for building digital twins (Digital Twin) in the development of architecture, security and cooperation rules of the digital twin with IT systems, which should accelerate the growth this technology. The consortium's goals are to create open source code, provide access to specialists and facilitate the building of conglomerates of companies that will deal with joint digital twin projects to reduce investment costs (Grendys, 2020).

Digital twin technologies are used, among others, by the CIECH Group, which cooperates with Siemens on a complete simulator of the soda production line. The creation of software that fully reflects soda ash production allowed technologists to search for ways to increase the efficiency of this process. The next step will enable the creation of a trainer for employees who are production operators. Thanks to this, they will be able to train in the production line operation and gain the qualifications necessary to manage the soda production process faster. The software, developed in 2019, also covers the functioning and parameters of the heat and power plant, which produces steam under high pressure, which is necessary for the production of soda. The simulator allows you to check the effect of changes in chemical and physical properties without the need to modify the actual operation. The tool works at the plant in Inowrocław, whose installations are reflected in the digital twin developed thanks to the Siemens gPROMS application. Based on the set parameters, the digital twin suggests, for example, how many and what raw materials to use to obtain the desired product (Grendys, 2022).

Another example of the use of digital twin is the American company specializing in producing and distributing electricity as well as air and rail transport – General Electric. Digital twins enable continuous monitoring of the operation of individual devices, for example, aircraft engines, gas and wind turbines in power plants. Thanks to machine learning, AI can predict the risk of failure and the associated potential costs. Based on simulations, the system can propose corrective actions, thanks to which the operation of a given plant can be optimized. The GE system is available in the computing cloud, Microsoft Azure and Amazon Web Services. Controlled devices can be previewed anytime with Microsoft HoloLens mixed reality goggles. A digital copy of a factory or their network allows you to test newly designed solutions, improve existing procedures and processes and be used to train employees.

An example is the use of digital twin technology to simulate the production processes of telecommunications satellites. OneWeb and Airbus have built two factories in Toulouse, France, and Merrit Island, USA. To meet the ambitious schedule to ship 900 telecommunications satellites, engineers used WITNESS Horizon software from US company Lannet to quickly run complex tests and manage satellite production. Ford also uses the WITNESS Horizon simulation tool to analyze and verify production in its factories (Tomczyk, 2020; Lanner, 2022).

Currently, more and more often, the support in the functioning of cyber-physical networks of enterprises is predictive simulation combined with a digital twin, which is an excellent tool for analyzing new projects. Especially in the recent period of disruptions in supply chains, operational planning has become more and more difficult. Predictive simulation and digital twins then assist decision-making by optimizing resource allocation and providing greater active control. A prime example is Mars Chocolate North America, which has 29 product lines operating in six US plants, each with a different product mix and volume requirements for chocolate produced. The quality standards adopted by the company limit the possibility of long-term storage. This means increased requirements for the accuracy of production planning and continuous analysis of operational efficiency based on different scenarios on individual lines and network locations. Using a digital twin supported by predictive simulation allowed to define the optimal way of working within the existing constraints while identifying previously unknown risks and enabling significant cost savings and efficiency improvements.

Bibliography

Abreu, A., & Camarinha-Matos, L. M. (2008). A benefit analysis model for collaborative networks. In L. M. Camarinha-Matos & H. Afsarmanesh (Eds.), *Collaborative networks reference modeling* (pp. 253–274). Springer.

Berger, R. (2016). *The Industrie 4.0 transition quantified. How the fourth industrial revolution is reshuffling the economic, social and industrial model.* Monachium: Roland Berger GmbH.

Blom, J., & Monk, A. (2003). Theory of personalisation of appearance: Why people personalise their mobile phones and PCs. *Human Computer Interaction, 18*(3).

Bosch-Sijtsema, P. M. (2003). *Virtualness, A new organizational dimension. The relationship between virtualness and knowledge.* s.n. https://research.rug.nl/en/publications/virtualness-a-new-organisational-dimension

Dunn, K. (2015). Globalization and consumer: What marketer needs to know. *The Neumann Business Review*, 16–30.

GE Digital. (2022). *Predix – Platforma IIoT*. Retrieved May 12, 2022, from www.vix.com.pl/produkty-ge-digital/predix-platforma-iiot/?gclid=Cj0KCQjw4PKTBhD8ARIsA

HChzRKyuK7G3ery6f_MRDIFcu3nmfUZ-UNRMrFN9YB3ZuV_NCBCUQ59i0waAu6JEALw_wcB

Grabowska, S., & Saniuk, S. (2021). Modern marketing for customized products under conditions of fourth industrial revolution. In J. Duda & A. Gąsior (Eds.), *Industry 4.0: A global perspective* (pp. 159–171). Taylor & Francis Group. https://doi.org/10.4324/9781003186373

Grendys, A. (2020). Digital twin consortium chce opracować standardy i słownictwo dla technologii cyfrowego bliźniaka. *Platforma Przemysłu Przyszłości*. Retrieved April 14, 2022, from https://przemyslprzyszlosci.gov.pl/digital-twin-consortium-chce-opracowac-standardy-i-slownictwo-dla-technologii-cyfrowego-blizniaka/

Grendys, A. (2022). Symulator linii produkcyjnej sody. *Platforma Przemysłu Przyszłości*. Retrieved April 14, 2022, from https://przemyslprzyszlosci.gov.pl/symulator-linii-produkcyjnej-sody/

Korena, Y., Shpitalnib, M., Guc, P., & Hu, S. (2015). Product design for mass-individualization. *Procedia CIRP*, Elsevier, *36*, 64–71.

Lanner. (2022). *WITNESS horizon 24.0*. Retrieved August 18, 2022, from www.lanner.com/en-us/insights/news/witness-horizon-24-0-now-available.html

Lies, J. (2017). Marketing 4.0 als Mittelstandskommunikation. In *Die Digitalisierung der Kommunikation im Mittelstand. essentials*. Springer.

Maresova, P., Soukal, I., Svobodova, L., Hedvicakova, M., Javanmardi, E., Selamat, A., & Krejcar, O. (2018). Consequences of industry 4.0. *Business and Economics. Economies*, *6*, 46.

Niehoff, S., & Beier, G. (2018). Industrie 4.0 and a sustainable development: A short study on the perception and expectations of experts in Germany. *International Journal of Innovation and Sustainable Development*, *12*(3).

Rodak, A. (2021). *Po co przedsiębiorstwom digital twin?Platforma przemysłu przyszłości*. https://przemyslprzyszlosci.gov.pl/po-co-firmom-digital-twin/

Romaniuk, K. (2013). *Społeczne uwarunkowania koopetycji przedsiębiorstw*. Uniwersytet Warmińsko-Mazurski.

Saniuk, S. (2022). Cyber-fizyczne sieci produkcyjne małych i średnich przedsiębiorstw zorientowane na spersonalizowaną produkcję. In R. Knosala (Ed.), *Inżynieria zarządzania: cyfryzacja produkcji. Aktualności badawcze 4* (pp. 63–72). Polskie Wydaw. Ekonomiczne (#).

Saniuk, S., Grabowska, S., & Gajdzik, B. (2020). Personalization of products in the industry 4.0 concept and its impact on achieving a higher level of sustainable consumption. *Energies*, *13*(22), 1–19. https://doi.org/10.3390/en13225895

Saniuk, S., & Saniuk, A. (2018). Decision support system for rapid production order planning in production network. In *The first international conference on intelligent systems in production engineering and maintenance – ISPEM* (Vol. 637, pp. 217–226). Springer International Publishing, Advances in Intelligent Systems and Computing. ISBN: 9783319644646

Senanayake, M. M., & Little, T. (2010). Mass customization: Points and extent of apparel customization. *Journal of Fashion Marketing and Management: An International Journal*, *14*(2), 282–299.

Stock, T., & Seliger, G. (2016). Opportunities of sustainable manufacturing in industry 4.0. Procedia CIRP 2016. *13th Global Conference on Sustainable Manufacturing – Decoupling Growth from Resource*, *40*, 536–541. https://doi.org/10.1016/j.procir.2016.01.129

Tomczyk, J. (2020). *Wszystko zostanie skopiowane – digital twin w fabryce, Platforma Przemysłu Przyszłości*. Retrieved March 13, 2020, from https://przemyslprzyszlosci.gov.pl/wszystko-zostanie-skopiowane-digital-twin-w-fabryce-przyszlosci/

Travica, B. (2014). *Examining the informing view of organization: Applying theoretical and managerial approaches*. IGI Global.

Travica, B. (2015). Modeling organizational intelligence: Nothing googles like google. *Online Journal of Applied Knowledge Management – A Publication of the International Institute for Applied Knowledge Management, 3*(2). www.iiakm.org/ojakm/articles/2015/volume3_2/OJAKM_Volume3_2pp1-18.pdf

Walters, D., & Buchanan, J. (2001). The new economy, new opportunities and new structures. *Management Decision, 39*(10), 822–823.

Zakrzewska-Bielawska, A. (2013). Koopetycja – strategią sukcesu? Doświadczenia przedsiębiorstw high-tech. *Zarządzanie i Finanse, 4*(1), 419–431.

5 The concept of Business Model 4.0

Business model – theoretical approach

The issue of building business models is of great scientific and research interest. The term "business model" was first used in 1960 by M. Jones to reflect the interaction between universities and business. More attention was paid to business models only after 1995. This was correlated with the proliferation of the Internet around the world in the context of identifying the growing profitability reserves of companies through the implementation of Internet technologies in their operations to create value for the consumer (Zott et al., 2011). The most commonly cited elements of the business model include the company's position in the value chain, customer value, revenue sources, competitive strategy, resources/competencies, relationships with partners, products offered, sustainability, open innovations and costs (Shakeel et al., 2020; Pieroni et al., 2019; Rachinger et al., 2018; Bocken et al., 2019; Lanzolla & Markides, 2021). Since a business model is supposed to create revenue, it therefore depends on the aforementioned elements. The business models developed and implemented by companies determine their profitability and competitiveness. New strategic behavior is determined by the changes that can be observed in modern business.

Today, managers are required to apply increasingly sophisticated management methods and concepts (Jabłoński & Jabłoński, 2020a). The progressive globalization and networking of the economy makes it necessary to create new concepts of doing business. Their theoretical detailing and at the same time the possibility of application are the concepts of business models, of which business processes are an important element. They represent, as it were, a way of realizing value in the form of relationships with customers, in particular, providing them with products that meet specific needs (Ranta et al., 2021). As key theses and principles of the business concept approach can be considered (Tucci et al., 2018):

- ensure the implementation of two functions fundamental to business and entrepreneurship (marketing and innovation);
- productive use of resources;

DOI: 10.4324/9781003317401-6

- the imperative to make a profit and its relationship to business risk;
- innovative creation of customer value and added value;
- obtaining a competitive position in the market.

A company's business model is presented as a set of activities, methods and the time to carry them out, using its resources to do so in such a way as to create the highest value for the customer and ensure that it is positioned to capture value. Innovation can be applied in all its elements and is necessary to create customer value (Tucci et al., 2018). It reflects the implementation of strategy in the perspective of economic effects. The role of strategy is exposed in the model, as current and future revenues are generated through products offered to customers, as well as competitive approaches to the market. What results consequently is a revenue stream and return on investment, obtained through a combination of profit margins and an appropriate cost structure (Spiegal et al., 2018).

The business model can also be understood as an organization's adoption of methods of augmenting and utilizing resources to present customers with an offer of products and services that by their value exceeds that of competitors and that at the same time ensures the organization's profitability. It is treated as one of the determinants affecting the efficiency of the enterprise. The author of this concept A. Afuah (2020) emphasizes the importance of the so-called change factor. This factor is identified with innovations, especially those of a disruptive nature. As a basic example of such innovation, the cited author mentions the opportunities created by the use of the Internet and e-tools. In doing so, he notes that breakthrough innovations indirectly, but significantly, affect the efficiency of a company.

Frank et al. (2019), on the other hand, point out that the business model is closely related to processes, and in particular to business processes, and therefore business management. A company's business model is a concept of how it – in the identified and diagnosed by it condition of the environment – intends to product its business. Its shape – the way – is a specific configuration of resources, activities and offered products or services, which ensures the creation of value for the customer and the generation of profit for the owners of the enterprise.

Thus, the business model will be a tool that contains a certain set of elements and relations between them, schematically representing the business idea and will be a static model of the phenomenon. Havrylenko et al. (2020), on the other hand, considers it a reflection of how to achieve the right economic results expressed by the relations of revenue, costs and profit in the area of the whole enterprise. This model directly corresponds to the so-called performance model, which determines the relationship between:

- the structure of the sector, due to the intensity of competition;
- the behavior of companies and participants in the sector;
- economic performance, obtained by the organization in comparison with its competitors.

Business models refer to how a company defines its competitive strategy through the design of the product or service it offers to the market, how it charges for it, how much it costs to produce, how it differentiates itself from other companies through value propositions and how a company integrates its own value chain with that of other companies (Lee & Jung, 2018).

Although very often the understanding of the model is intuitive – it is nevertheless determined by very specific, strategic dimensions called key dimensions, which include (Chauhan & Singh, 2021):

- customer selection;
- value capture;
- differentiation (strategic control);
- scope of operations.

Osterwalder et al. (2020) provide a definition of a business model as a model that describes the determinants that interact to create value and to provide and profit from that created value. The value proposition offered to customers is, in addition to resources, competencies and external relationships. It is also one of the basic elements of a business model, which is a new conceptual tool that contains a set of documents and reactions between them that depict the logic of a given enterprise in a specific field (business). It contains a description of the value offered by the enterprise to a group or groups of customers, with the identification of the basic resources, processes (activities), as well as external relations of this enterprise, offering and delivering value and ensuring the enterprise's competitiveness in a particular field and enabling it to increase its value.

Newth, on the other hand, distinguishes value proposition, value chain and revenue as components of a business model. According to the author, when creating a business model, the key is to find answers to the questions: What does the enterprise offer to customers? Who is the enterprise's customer? What is the value proposition? Why does the business model generate revenue? Figure 5.1 shows the components of a business model according to Newth.

The business model is not the same as the organization's strategy and therefore should not be equated with it, despite the fact that there are important similarities and relationships between these concepts. Strategy and business model are not the same, but they are mutually dependent. The business model shapes strategy, because for a strategy to be viable, it must be based on a company's capabilities, resources and existing position (Braun et al., 2019). Table 5.1 shows a comparison of business model and strategy by selected criteria.

The business model allows verification, a kind of "check" of the organization's strategy. It is sometimes treated as a supplement, a detailing of the strategy, or as a concept that includes the strategy (primarily competitive). The business model makes it possible to test it in the context of other important elements of the organization, such as the architecture of the organization's value chain or the nature of strategic resources (Drzewiecki, 2018).

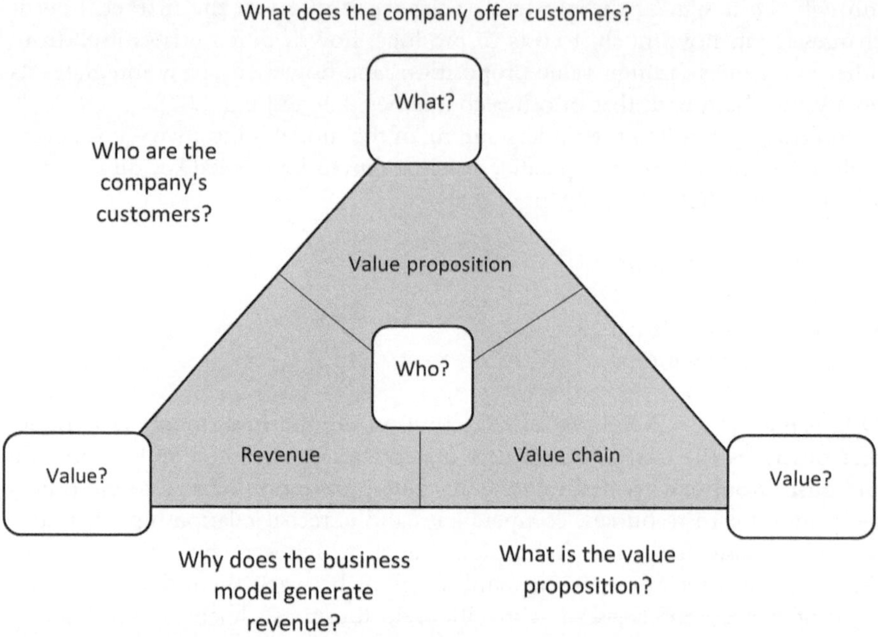

Figure 5.1 Components of the business model according to Newth

Source: Authors' elaboration.

Table 5.1 Business model and strategy – comparison by selected criteria

Business model	*Strategy*
Elements (design)	
Defined structure. Depending on how it is framed, it can include a diverse set of elements including the interior of the organization, as well as its environment, partners, value chain elements, technical architecture elements, social architecture elements, open innovation and so on.	In classical terms, it includes the goals of the enterprise, the means (tools) and their implementation plan. It may include information on ways of competitive struggle, behavior in relation to competitors, mission, vision and so on.
Desired characteristics	
Matching internally and externally, the various elements should be consistent and support each other. Their characteristics are innovation and durability, resilience and flexibility.	Fit with other elements of the organization and the situation in the sector.
The course of formulation	
More often, proceedings of an intuitive nature, emphasized the importance of learning, experience, cooperation and so on. Interactive nature of processes.	Fit with other elements of the organization and the situation in the sector.

(*Continued*)

Table 5.1 (Continued)

Business model	*Strategy*
Formalization	
As a rule, the effect is not formalized, alternatively, some elements are formalized.	The result is often a formal document that can be accessed by all employees of the company and often by all stakeholders in the company's environment.
Generality level	
The business model encompasses the entire organization, with strategy in many approaches to the business model.	Level of organization.
Creating value/achieving competitive advantage	
Focus on value creation and generating, and protecting, profits.	Focus on achieving a competitive advantage in the sector.
Method of use	
A strategic planning and management tool to help construct a business plan, it serves as a comprehensive comparison of enterprises.	First and foremost, a tool for corporate planning and strategic management.

Source: Authors' elaboration.

The business model should change with the volatility of the market and the interior of the company or even anticipate market expectations, even create them. Managers should perform the so-called fine-tuning of the business model (Jablonski & Jablonski, 2020). Thus, the business model must have certain characteristics that make this fine-tuning possible. Table 5.2 shows five characteristics that a business model should have. They are integrity, consistency, openness, flexibility and effectiveness.

Table 5.2 Key features of modern business models

Feature name	*Description of the feature*
Integrity	The components of the model are defined and form a coherent whole
Consistency	Close and compatible connection of business model components with each other and with the environment
Openness	Creating interactions with the environment
Flexibility	Configuration of the components
Effectiveness	Leads to the intended effect of the goal

Source: Authors' elaboration.

Business models focused on the process of creating competitiveness, innovation and value

Competition in the economy plays an important role and is one of the important areas of interest in management theory and practice. The functioning of enterprises in competitive conditions determines the directions of development and creates the types of strategy and business models adopted. Continuous market rivalry among enterprises results in the search for sources of obtaining competitive advantage, aimed at maintaining or improving the existing position in the market (Jabłoński &Jabłoński, 2020b). Observing the transformations taking place in the economy, we notice a steady increase in the importance of information resources against material or financial resources. The sources of a company's success in a competitive market are seen in an efficient, effective management system and in the attitude of managers who quickly make accurate decisions. The basis of all decisions is information and in particular information about the company's environment (Jelonek et al., 2018).

Porter's (2001) body of work on competitiveness has been significantly applied to the conceptualization of business models. It should be noted that the focus has been on that part of this author's theoretical achievements that deal with the microeconomic view of a company's competitiveness; hence, the model that determines national competitive advantages, called the "rhombus of national advantage" or the "diamond of national competitive advantage," for example, has not been considered. It is certainly worthwhile to present, if only in a synthetic way, the views of this author, which directly relate to the formation of competitive strategy, which, in combination with operational efficiency, constitutes a certain model of the enterprise's activities, ensuring its economic success, which is also an important component of business models. The presentation of Porter's (2001) views on this issue can begin with the thesis he puts forward: strategy and operational efficiency are conditions for obtaining the most important goal of the enterprise, which is its economic performance.

However, this author concludes that each of these determinants (and therefore strategy and operational efficiency) interacts differently to achieve this goal. An introductory, but important issue for the transparency of the concept presented is the distinction between strategy and operational efficiency. The trend toward increased efficiency, quality and speed in conducting operations has led to the emergence and application of such management techniques and tools as, for example, benchmarking, outsourcing, TQM, supplier partnerships and reengineering. All such concepts, which are increasingly widely used, are treated by Porter as elements of operational efficiency, not ensuring long-term profitability for the company. The author claims that currently there is significantly less appreciation of the importance of strategy. In particular, it is about its core, which is the competitive position of the enterprise in the market. In his view, a company will only manage to outperform its competitors if it can differentiate itself in a sustainable way. Thus, it should deliver more value to customers or provide comparable value at a lower cost, or both. Such action leads to increased profitability by achieving higher prices in the market or through greater efficiency, lowering average unit costs. As a result, all differences between companies in terms of costs or prices arise from the activities necessary to develop, produce, sell and deliver their products or services. Costs are created by performing activities, so lower costs are achieved by performing individual activities more efficiently than competitors do. Gaining a competitive advantage in the market involves performing:

- activities that are different from those of competitors, so to speak, original, carried out exclusively by a given enterprise;
- activities similar to those of competitors in a different way.

Competitive strategy is about pursuing unique activities that enable you to differentiate yourself (Salunke et al., 2019). This means consciously choosing a set of activities that bring a certain set of values, enabling you to retain existing customers and attract new ones. In the operational sphere part, the advantage comes from the ability to more effectively and efficiently carry out activities typical of the business, therefore similar to those of the competition. Measures of such activities can be, for example: efficiency and effectiveness in the use of resources obtained, among other things, through improved quality or faster development of new products. It is also worth noting this author's interesting point of view regarding competition based on operational efficiency (Desyllas et al., 2018). The techniques used to achieve operational efficiency, as mentioned previously, cause companies to be so similar that one can speak of a convergence of competition that is devastating to companies. This destruction can only be stopped by reducing rivalry, which is facilitated by the cooperation of enterprises in a cyber-physical network, in which competitors become business partners working together to fulfill a common order (Panetto et al., 2019).

The need to constantly improve strategy or even reinvent it is an important element in shaping a company's competitive advantage. One can then speak of cases of strategic continuity. An enterprise should use its core of uniqueness if it modifies or redefines its strategic management model. The core of uniqueness can be identified by answering the following questions (Brzóska, 2018):

- Which of the enterprise's products and services stand out the most?
- Which of the company's products and services are most profitable?
- Which of the enterprise's customers (customer groups) are most satisfied?
- Which customers, distribution channels or places to buy are most profitable?
- Which activities in the enterprise's value chain stand out the most and are the most effective?

In terms of the theory of competition, one can observe the evolution that takes place on the basis of evolution. What can be observed in the market, and what is at the heart of the competitive game, should be taken as a starting point in the discussion of the competitiveness of the enterprise. Without competition, there is no problem of competitiveness. Enterprise competitiveness is defined as the ability of enterprises to sustain their base of satisfying the needs of customers and consumers through a more efficient supply of goods and services on increasingly better price and non-price terms – better than competitors (Gorynia, 2018). This definition clearly exposes the element of relating the characteristics of the object whose competitiveness we are studying to those of other objects. This means that competitiveness is a relative characteristic, that is, one whose meaning presupposes some type of relationship linking the object about which we are judging something with other objects.

New business concepts are translated into a concrete model that provides the strategic and operational basis for changing the configuration of products and processes in the company. Competitive business models, to a significantly greater extent than, for example, new technologies, change the existing competitive configuration, often shattering the status quo. Most often, the arena for such radical changes are companies and sectors considered to be modern (information technology, telecommunications, pharmaceutical industry) (Grabowska & Saniuk, 2022a).

In today's difficult, especially economic, conditions, product or process innovations alone seem to be insufficient. Turoń (2022) argues that only innovation in the area of the entire business model can save a company in times of crisis and ensure its continued growth. Experimenting with new business models now seems to be an important competence for a company that wants to succeed in innovating (Bogers et al., 2019).

Research in the field of innovative business models has developed independently of the emergence of a comprehensive theory of business models. An innovative business model is generally defined as a process to reduce costs, optimize processes, access new markets or improve financial performance. Compared to product and process innovations, an innovative business model consists of a systemic change that affects the value of businesses, the proposition and how that value is generated. If the implementation of an innovative business model is successful, the innovation process should lead to a positive transformation and renewal of the enterprise. The development of an innovative business model is usually spurred by a change in the competitive environment, such as the pressure caused by the introduction of a new disruptive technology. Such transformation is supported by the choices of decision-makers who monitor the evolution of the company's business model to understand how to stimulate innovation in the sector (Botelho et al., 2021; Huang et al., 2021; Jabbour et al., 2020).

The development of an effective business model creates the threat of imitation by competitors. The distance between competing companies can quickly shrink due to the impermanence of competitive advantages or the streamlining of business models by competitors. In such a situation, there is a need for continuous improvement of business models (the so-called "running ahead"). This can be achieved through partial or breakthrough innovations. Partial innovations involve changes within the existing model. They are expressed by building advantages, for example, in the areas of product quality, distribution network, sales network, research and development, customer relations (CRM) or production processes.

Introducing disruptive innovation is the second way of "running ahead." It involves shaping the value chain in such a novel way that an innovation is created that starts a wave of creative destruction in the market, leading to the creation of a completely new business model. It is worth noting that the presented views on innovation correspond with the approach presented by Tucci (2022) to the role of disruptive change in building business models. According to the author of the concept under discussion, regardless of whether we deal with the mutation of an existing business model or create a completely new one with the goal of creating and retaining value in the market, we always operate on the same material. Its elements are:

- competitive advantage;
- resources and skills;
- value chain.

Companies that want to succeed in the market must operate in such a way as to generate added value for the customer. Value is seen in a unique business model, dynamic capabilities, innovation, strategic potential of the organization or organizational entrepreneurship. The ability of a business organization to create value in the broadest sense is seen as one of the essential conditions for achieving and maintaining competitive advantage. As a result, the spectrum of value management in question is becoming wider and wider, covering activities in the areas of marketing, investment, finance, human resources, quality, cooperation and, above all, innovation – including the pillars of Industry 4.0. In this context, an important issue is the search for such management methods and instruments that enable value creation. The value obtained determines to a large extent whether the business model will be effective in achieving the organization's goals and its economic, market and social effects. Also, it indicates its ability to implement various types of innovations that co-create both customer value and growth in the economic value (economic profit and resources) of the enterprise. Value in an enterprise's business model has a fundamental role. It is the essence of the company's existence and the factor through which it is possible to ensure the satisfaction of shareholders who take business risks but also of the various stakeholder groups participating in all its activities; it determines and is a confirmation of the effectiveness and efficiency of the business model. A business model focused on value creation answers the questions posed by Peter Drucker: who is the customer? What value is the customer? It also answers the basic questions that every manager must ask: How do we make money in this business? What is the basic economic logic that explains how we can deliver value to customers at the right cost (Andreassen et al., 2018)?

Amit and Zott (2020) distinguish four primary sources of value creation that can be applied to the business model:

1 Efficiency. The increase in efficiency in the network is caused by the reduction of asymmetries in access to information, as well as the ability to make faster decisions additionally on the basis of a larger pool of information. Reduced distribution costs and reduced inventory management costs are also sources of efficiency improvements.

2 Complementarity. The source of value, according to resource theory, can be the complementarity of strategic resources. This includes situations where complementary goods are supplied to the customer by a competitor.
3 Maintenance. The potential for value creation in a business is greater the more customers are motivated to repeat their transactions and the greater the determination of both parties to the transaction to sustain and strengthen the relationship. This potential can be realized through the "retention" effect, which most often manifests itself in the form of higher migration costs for customers and strategic partners to competitors. The source of significant retention benefits is usually the offering of a specific product, service or, more broadly, customer value for the first time.
4 Innovation. New products or services, new methods of production, distribution and marketing have traditionally been seen as sources of value creation. The development of information technology means that increasingly the source of value is the innovative structuring of transactions between stakeholders. Bringing together entities that have not previously exchanged with each other (pro-products, services, information and so on) can lead, for example, to lower transaction costs, identify dormant consumer needs and incorporate complementary products/services into the value proposition.

An enterprise selects and allocates its customers according to the products or services it offers, trying to best match its offerings to their needs. Through networking, enterprises significantly increase their potential and ability to meet customer needs. The value capture dimension of the model, in turn, describes how value is created for customers, as well as how they are rewarded for delivering it. Traditionally, companies captured value by selling products or receiving payment for services provided. Today, companies use a much broader repertoire of value capture mechanisms, such as by extending the value chain, offering complementary products and services or sharing value. Value capture is related to ways of making profit.

Progressive globalization and rapid technological advances are creating a digital economy, with their influence extending to both the production and communication spheres – radically changing the business environment of companies. In particular, the relationship between the manufacturer (supplier) and the customer (recipient) is changing. The customer has incomparably more choices; the variants of the offer prepared for him are available quickly and transparently. Companies must therefore be increasingly customer-oriented, systematically reviewing the values (value propositions) provided to the customer. The changing business environment is intensifying the need not only to adapt the company's offerings to the customer's needs but also to revise the approach to both value creation and partial appropriation. This translates into the need to revise the business models previously used by companies. The ability to define and redefine an enterprise's business model should be counted among the key competencies that foster enterprise value creation (To et al., 2020).

Architecture of Business Model 4.0

Business Model 4.0 is defined as a configuration of business processes that connect and develop resources, shaped in the form of an enterprise social and technical architecture, with a focus on sustainability. The architecture of this model is built on resilient processes, enabling cyber-physical networking that can meet the demand for personalized products.

The Business 4.0 model is based on a strong combination of the megatrends of the Fourth Industrial Revolution and the pillars of Industry 4.0. The implementation of strategies in the Business 4.0 model in practice is carried out through the construction of cyber-physical collaboration networks, ensuring both the efficient use of resources and skills, as well as their renewal and process resilience. The technological innovations being implemented enable cyber-physical collaboration networks to produce personalized products and offer complementary services. These activities take into account the principles of sustainable production.

Figure 5.2 shows the layout of the determinants of competitive advantage of the Business 4.0 model. The key elements affecting the competitive advantage of this model are the megatrends of the Fourth Industrial Revolution and the pillars of Industry 4.0. The megatrends of industrial revolution are Economy

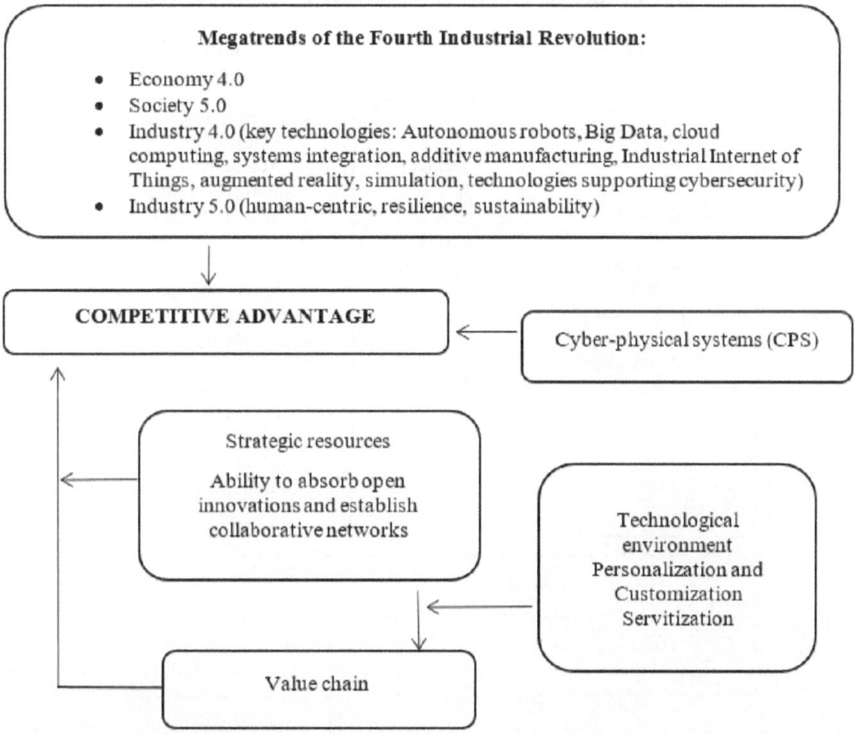

Figure 5.2 Layout of determinants of competitive advantage of Business Model 4.0

Source: Authors' elaboration.

4.0, Society 5.0, Industry 4.0 and Industry 5.0. Also influencing competitive advantage are cyber-physical CPS, value chain and technological environment, personalization, customization and servitization. At the center of the layout of the determinants of the Business 4.0 model are placed strategic resources, the ability to absorb innovation and the ability to establish cooperation.

The Business Model 4.0 is based on a configuration of social architecture and technical architecture linked by resilient business processes. The model clearly exposes the role of business processes, which are supported by the pillars of Industry 4.0 and Industry 5.0. The model is influenced by the megatrends of the Fourth Industrial Revolution and customers. The model exposes the competitors and stakeholders. Partners forming a cyber-physical network (CPS) are also a very important element. Figure 5.3 shows the architecture of the Business Model 4.0.

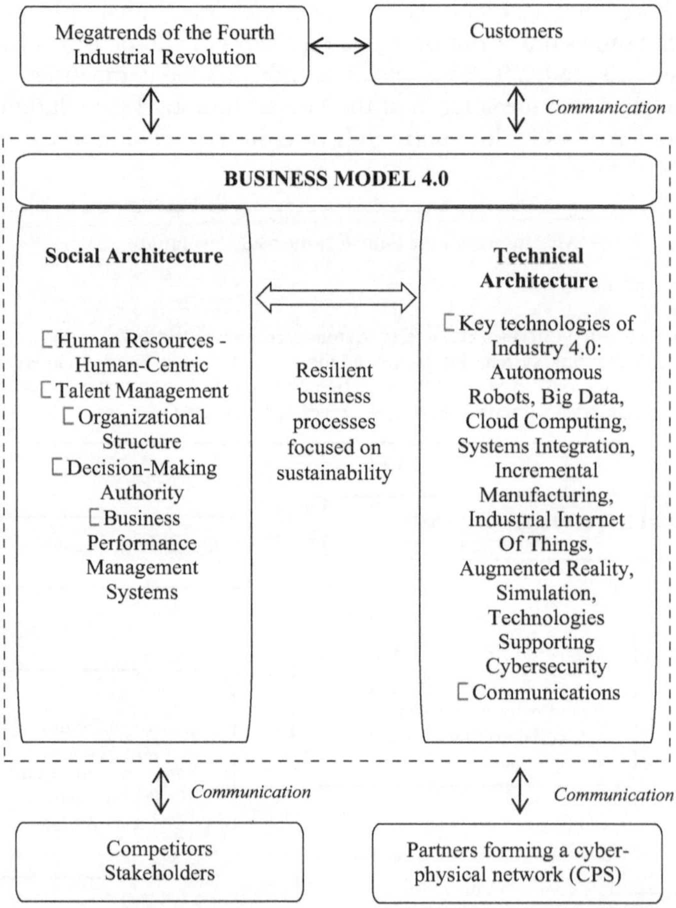

Figure 5.3 Business Model 4.0 – Architecture

Source: Authors' elaboration.

The technical architecture of Business Model 4.0 encompasses the pillars of Industry 4.0. This enables the concept of Business Model 4.0 for a smart enterprise, a partner, forming a cyber-physical collaboration network (CPS). The technical architecture of the Business Model 4.0 enables CPS systems to collect data, process it and interact with the physical processes occurring throughout the production network, thanks to the unlimited interconnection of a network of intelligent, mechatronic resources (machines, equipment, robots, means of transportation etc.) communicating with each other, with a human being acting as supervisor and/or coordinator.

The foundation of this architecture is communication, allowing machines and sensors to transmit data not only among themselves but also directly with Ethernet or the cloud. Closed systems are becoming open systems. In the future, using decentralized computing power, data will be transformed into information directly in the sensor. Decisions will be made at a decentralized level. Process, production and enterprise information will be transferred directly to Ethernet and the cloud. Maximizing the digitization of the technical architecture is to increase machine availability, increase manufacturing speed, increase product quality, increase production flexibility and increase the level of safety for employees, who remain at the center of the enterprise, according to the Industry 5.0 concept. The technical architecture will rapidly absorb the latest technological solutions, supporting the ability to personalize production while keeping mass-produced products competitively priced (Grabowska & Saniuk, 2022b).

The social architecture of this model is human-centric, human resources, talent management, organizational structure, decision-making authority and corporate performance management systems. As the Fourth Industrial Revolution creates a new work environment and labor market conditions, an important component of this architecture will be competency management and talent management within the company. The automation and digitization of business, as well as the need to constantly adapt to the changing environment of the enterprise, requires completely new competencies of the workforce and therefore a change or reorganization of the social architecture of the business model. Therefore, for the fourth-generation industry, it is crucial not only to attract talent from the labor market but first and foremost to develop skills among the employed workforce, which should be a strategic goal of any smart enterprise. Such measures make it possible to spot staff shortages or gaps in employees' competencies in time and enable the implementation of corrective measures. These, in turn, include not only classical training, but also the rotation of employees between teams, enabling engineers to plan their own career paths or including them in the process of shaping the vision of the company's development. After all, in smart companies, it is necessary to keep in mind the soft competencies of employees, which so far have not been required of engineers. The ability to cooperate, communicate, empathize, be creative or take responsibility for their own actions will determine the success of a smart enterprise.

In a Smart Factory environment, employees who are able to interact with others to accomplish common tasks, in the process of creating value for the company, are valuable. In addition to the obvious area of specific knowledge, updated and acquired by engineers on an ongoing basis, it is also important to create the so-called soft skills of engineers, such as how to implement tasks and projects, problem solving and teamwork. The combination of these elements makes it possible to distinguish specialists who are able to adapt to the work culture and way of functioning in modern factories. Even today, qualities such as openness to change, efficiency and flexibility are particularly desirable (Saniuk et al., 2022). These are also what engineers learn in the workplace thanks to the availability of special programs in the organization to shape and develop these competencies. Certainly, within the social architecture of the Business 4.0 model, quite a few changes will be made in human resource management, collaboration or interpersonal communication.

In management theory, we have the classical division of labor, the formal authority of the manager, the unity of command and management, the subordination of personal interests to the general interest and hierarchy and organizational structures are the guarantors of effective organizational management. The Fourth Industrial Revolution imposes new conditions and styles of work. The management of the social architecture of the Business Model 4.0 is moving toward the concept of a turquoise organization, which in its assumptions assumes both the absence of a hierarchical system and a formal incentive system. For, from the point of view of operational efficiency, functions performed rather than positions held are of greater importance in turquoise organizations, and self-regulation and self-management are of greater value in the process of evolution and achievement of business goals (Grabowska, 2020).

An important aspect of the social architecture of Business Model 4.0 will be trust. It will be the key to the success of the enterprise. Employees will have a real impact on the development of the company, they will perform functions tailored to their potential and competencies, and their change will come not from coercion but from their own motivation based on competence development or the desire to "prove themselves" in new conditions. The key will be to preserve and maintain a balance between the intrinsic motivation of employees and an appropriate work environment in which people in their approach are aware and convinced that being members of the organization, they are responsible for it, and by engaging in various tasks tailored to their individual competencies, they consciously use their potential, creating value in the process. This will require creating a friendly and safe work environment in which employees feel equal and respected (Demir et al., 2019).

Smart factories creating a Business Model 4.0 should be organizations with a flat organizational structure, where employees develop, share knowledge and experience, and support each other in performing specific tasks/functions. In such companies, communication and an efficient information flow system become key, as well as the creation of a space where employees can openly share knowledge, exchange lessons learned, generate ideas and make proposals for improvement activities, and can collaborate with robots. Such a space increases each employee's sense of purpose and impact on the company's operations, thereby stimulating innovation and development.

Modifying the way and style of communication within social architecture can be most challenging because it means working to change existing habits and standards. It also means changing the optics of how mistakes occur, focusing on lessons learned from mistakes, where the communication and feedback process is constructive, devoid of judgmental elements and focused on innovation and development rather than implementing a cycle of discipline. Also different is the role and expectations of managers, who turn into leaders and mentors, becoming Leaders 4.0. Organizations that manage all processes, with a fluid (unstructured) flow of resources and a flexible approach to taking on roles that are defined by members of the organization on an ongoing basis, depending on current needs taking into account the predispositions of individuals and the talents of each employee, may better fit the expectations of the work of representatives of generations Y and Z.

Another cornerstone of the Business Model 4.0 is business processes, which are the means of creating value for customers, in particular, providing them with products and/or services that meet specific needs. Business processes are a combination of social architecture and technical architecture while at the same time deriving from them the resources necessary to realize appropriate products that create value for the customer, often personalized. Key principals in the design of business processes of the Business Model 4.0 have been identified. Business processes are characterized by:

- interoperability – creating communication standards between enterprises, cyber-physical systems and human teams;
- virtualization – creating virtual work/collaboration/cooperation models and simulation models;
- decentralization – handing over decisions on how to manufacture smart products, with full electronic tracking of the entire value chain at the same time;
- resilience – high resistance to disruptions and market changes caused by global crises;
- real-time decision-making capability – access to all key process information automatically, based on data downloaded from machines and equipment;
- service orientation – opening up the use of assets (factories, technology, human teams) for service use for other factories, as well as for servitization;
- orientation to personalization of production – providing the customer with a product maximally tailored to his needs;
- orientation to servitization – increasing the proportion of services in the company's portfolio;
- orientation to sustainable production – production linked to the concept of reducing the use of resources and the environmental impact of a product, from design to end of life.

By absorbing the pillars of Industry 4.0, the Business Model 4.0 significantly creates value through their use. This gives the ability to monetize value, making the Business Model 4.0 informationally innovative. Various analysis techniques are also setting new trends in big data. These include data mining techniques, large online repositories, visualization methods, machine learning, optimization methods, social network analysis, among others. These methods enhance the operational functionality of processes. Variety, speed of processing, size of data, reliability of data, value of data – determine the assumptions of shaping Business Model 4.0 based on access and use of data. The technical architecture of the Business 4.0 model is built on the pillars of Industry 4.0, which support value creation throughout the value chain. Table 5.3 shows the impact of the Industry 4.0 pillars on value creation throughout its chain.

Analyzing Table 5.3, it can be pointed out that autonomous robots increase process efficiency, production efficiency and flexibility, reduce manufacturing costs and increase safety for workers. Big Data makes it possible to reduce

Table 5.3 Impact of Industry 4.0 pillars on value creation in Business Model 4.0

Pillar of Industry 4.0	*Value creation*
Autonomous robots	• Increase in process efficiency • Increase in production efficiency • Decrease in the cost of manufacturing • Increase in process flexibility • Increase in safety for employees
Big Data	• Reduction of infrastructure costs (by outsourcing) • Guarantee of data security against cyberattack • Ability to use additional services of advanced analytics and AI (machine learning)
Systems integration	• Efficient flow of information and data between production and business systems • Creating a network of cooperating companies • Reducing delivery times for personalized orders • Accelerate decision-making processes between teams • Increase profitability
Additive manufacturing	• Reducing prototyping costs • Reducing storage costs
Industrial Internet of Things	• Creation of reliable information on the progress of processes • Unlimited (time and place) access to information • Increased quality of personalized products
Augmented and virtual reality	• Time and cost savings in the physical preparation of new product prototypes • Reduced deployment time for new employees • Increased work safety • Reduction in operating costs • Reducing the cost of deploying new employees
Simulations	
Technologies to support cybersecurity	• Protecting data, information, networks from cyberattacks and unauthorized access

Source: Authors' elaboration.

infrastructure costs, is a guarantee of data security against cyberattacks and provides the opportunity to use additional services of advanced analytics and AI. Systems integration, in turn, is an efficient flow of information that enables the creation of cyber-physical networks of cooperating enterprises, which consequently increases profitability. With additive manufacturing, companies reduce prototyping and warehousing costs. The Industrial Internet of Things gives unlimited access to information, which has a direct impact on increasing the quality of personalized products. Augmented and virtual reality and simulations support the induction of new employees, employee training, and enhance workplace safety. Meanwhile, technologies supporting cyber security ensure that data, information and networks are protected from cyberattacks.

Value creation through the Business Model 4.0 is emphasized through:

- the value proposition, that is, the value created for customers through a specific offering of personalized products and complementary services;
- defining the target market segment and the specification of the revenue generation mechanism (i.e., it defines the audience of the offering and the reason why they will be interested in the offering);
- defining the structure of the value chain required for the creation and distribution of the offer and the complementary resources necessary to support the position in the value network;
- detailing the mechanisms by which the company will receive payment for the offer delivered and thus earn revenue;
- determination of the cost of fulfilling the offer and the level of profit that can be obtained;
- determination of the enterprise's position in the value network;
- formulating the assumptions of a competitive strategy to achieve and maintain a competitive advantage over rivals.

The Business Model 4.0 singles out the customer as the main element of a company's strategic values. At this point, it should be noted that the customer is willing to pay for needs that he consciously expects but also for such elements that he has not consciously identified. This is why so much attention in the Business 4.0 model is devoted to personalization. The company's task is to provide a value proposition that not only responds to the customer's reported demand but also comes up with future, complementary values. Their correct identification and offer to the customer is the most important bond between the customer and the manufacturer, this affects the length and durability of the customer–enterprise relationship, which, in turn, translates into the competitiveness of the enterprise's business model.

A successful enterprise Business Model 4.0 that achieves long-term profitability should be based on the following elements of competitive advantage:

- a strategy that enables sustainable competitive advantage, which is constantly monitored and based on the megatrends of the fourth industrial revolution;

- a management system that ensures operational efficiency through competitive business processes built on the pillars of Industry 4.0.

These are the two main components of the model, except that it treats their role and the way they are shaped differently. The basis of the strategy is the strategic (competitive) position achieved by the enterprise, which results from the value offered to customers and the selection and configuration of appropriate activities. The formation of this position is an essential, overarching and innovative part of the model, a condition that determines the long-term profitability of the enterprise.

Bibliography

Afuah, A. (2020). Forgotten scientific miracles. *Ross School of Business Paper* (1399).

Amit, R., & Zott, C. (2020). *Business model innovation strategy: Transformational concepts and tools for entrepreneurial leaders*. John Wiley & Son Ltd.

Andreassen, T. W., Lervik-Olsen, L., Snyder, H., Van Riel, A. C., Sweeney, J. C., & Van Vaerenbergh, Y. (2018). Business model innovation and value-creation: The triadic way. *Journal of Service Management, 29*, 883–906. https://doi.org/10.1108/josm-05-2018-0125

Bocken, N., Boons, F., & Baldassarre, B. (2019). Sustainable business model experimentation by understanding ecologies of business models. *Journal of Cleaner Production, 208*, 1498–1512.

Bogers, M., Chesbrough, H., Heaton, S., & Teece, D. J. (2019). Strategic management of open innovation: A dynamic capabilities perspective. *California Management Review, 62*(1), 77–94.

Botelho, D. F., Dias, B. H., de Oliveira, L. W., Soares, T. A., Rezende, I., & Sousa, T. (2021). Innovative business models as drivers for prosumers integration-Enablers and barriers. *Renewable and Sustainable Energy Reviews, 144*, 111057.

Braun, M., Latham, S., & Cannatelli, B. (2019). Strategy and business models: Why winning companies need both. *Journal of Business Strategy, 40*(5), 39–45. https://doi.org/10.1108/JBS-01-2019-0005

Brzóska, J. (2018). Koncepcje tworzenia wartości a zmiany modeli biznesu. *Zeszyty Naukowe. Organizacja i Zarządzanie/Politechnika Śląska*. https://www-arch.polsl.pl/wydzialy/ROZ/ZN/Documents/z%20121a/Brz%c3%b3ska.pdf

Chauhan, H., & Singh, A. K. (2021). Canvassing competitive advantage through key dimensions of business model. *International Journal of Business and Globalisation, 29*(2), 149–162.

Demir, K. A., Döven, G., & Sezen, B. (2019). Industry 5.0 and human-robot co-working. *Procedia Computer Science, 158*, 688–695.

Desyllas, P., Miozzo, M., Lee, H. F., & Miles, I. (2018). Capturing value from innovation in knowledge-intensive business service firms: The role of competitive strategy. *British Journal of Management, 29*(4), 769–795.

Drzewiecki, J. (2018). Outsourcing a wartość w modelach biznesu polskich przedsiębiorstw – wyniki badań. *Studia Ekonomiczne, 351*, 74–84.

Frank, A. G., Mendes, G. H., Ayala, N. F., & Ghezzi, A. (2019). Servitization and industry 4.0 convergence in the digital transformation of product firms: A business model innovation perspective. *Technological Forecasting and Social Change, 141*, 341–351.

Gorynia, M. (2018). Współczesne nauki ekonomiczne – tożsamość, ewolucja, klasyfikacje. *Ekonomista, 5*, 497–522.

Grabowska, S. (2020). Changes in the social architecture of business model in the perspective of the industry 4.0 concept. *Management, 24*(1).

Grabowska, S., & Saniuk, S. (2022a). Business models in the industry 4.0 environment – Results of web of science bibliometric analysis. *Journal of Open Innovation: Technology, Market, and Complexity, 8*(1), 19.

Grabowska, S., & Saniuk, S. (2022b). Development of business models in the fourth industrial revolution: Conditions in the context of empirical research on worldwide scope companies located in Poland. *Journal of Open Innovation: Technology, Market, and Complexity, 8*(2), 86.

Havrylenko, M., Shiyko, V., Horal, L., Khvostina, I., & Yashcheritsyna, N. (2020). Economic and mathematical modeling of industrial enterprise business model financial efficiency estimation. In *E3S web of conferences* (Vol. 166, p. 13025). EDP Sciences.

Huang, Y., Qian, L., Soopramanien, D., & Tyfield, D. (2021). Buy, lease, or share? Consumer preferences for innovative business models in the market for electric vehicles. *Technological Forecasting and Social Change, 166*, 120639.

Jabbour, C. J. C., Seuring, S., de Sousa Jabbour, A. B. L., Jugend, D., Fiorini, P. D. C., Latan, H., & Izeppi, W. C. (2020). Stakeholders, innovative business models for the circular economy and sustainable performance of firms in an emerging economy facing institutional voids. *Journal of Environmental Management, 264*, 110416.

Jabłoński, A., & Jabłoński, M. (2020a). New economy business models in the concepts of big data, the sharing economy and the circular economy. In *Social business models in the digital economy* (pp. 51–88). Palgrave Macmillan.

Jabłoński, A., & Jabłoński, M. (2020b). *Social business models in the digital economy*. Palgrave Macmillan.

Jelonek, D., Stępniak, C., & Ziora, L. (2018, April). The meaning of big data in the support of managerial decisions in contemporary organizations: Review of selected research. In *Future of information and communication conference* (pp. 361–368). Springer.

Lanzolla, G., & Markides, C. (2021). A business model view of strategy. *Journal of Management Studies, 58*(2), 540–553.

Lee, M. J., & Jung, J. S. (2018). Competitive strategy for paradigm shift in the era of the fourth industrial revolution: Focusing on business model innovation. *Indian Journal of Public Health Research & Development, 9*(8).

Newth, F. (2012). *Business models and strategic management. A new integration*. Business Expert Press.

Osterwalder, A., Pigneur, Y., Smith, A., & Etiemble, F. (2020). *The invincible company: How to constantly reinvent your organization with inspiration from the world's best business models, 4.* John Wiley & Sons.

Panetto, H., Iung, B., Ivanov, D., Weichhart, G., & Wang, X. (2019). Challenges for the cyber-physical manufacturing enterprises of the future. *Annual Reviews in Control, 47*, 200–213.

Pieroni, M. P., McAloone, T. C., & Pigosso, D. C. (2019). Business model innovation for circular economy and sustainability: A review of approaches. *Journal of Cleaner Production, 215*, 198–216.

Porter, M. (2001). *Porter o konkurencji*. Polskie Wydawnictwo Ekonomiczne.

Rachinger, M., Rauter, R., Müller, C., Vorraber, W., & Schirgi, E. (2018). Digitalization and its influence on business model innovation. *Journal of Manufacturing Technology Management*. https://doi.org/10.1108/JMTM-01-2018-0020

Ranta, V., Aarikka-Stenroos, L., & Väisänen, J. M. (2021). Digital technologies catalyzing business model innovation for circular economy – Multiple case study. *Resources, Conservation and Recycling, 164*, 105155.

Salunke, S., Weerawardena, J., & McColl-Kennedy, J. R. (2019). The central role of knowledge integration capability in service innovation-based competitive strategy. *Industrial Marketing Management*, *76*, 144–156.

Saniuk, S., Grabowska, S., & Straka, M. (2022). Identification of social and economic expectations: Contextual reasons for the transformation process of industry 4.0 into the industry 5.0 concept. *Sustainability*, *14*(3), 1391.

Shakeel, J., Mardani, A., Chofreh, A. G., Goni, F. A., & Klemeš, J. J. (2020). Anatomy of sustainable business model innovation. *Journal of Cleaner Production*, *261*, 121201.

Spiegal, S., Bestelmeyer, B. T., Archer, D. W., Augustine, D. J., Boughton, E. H., Boughton, R. K., . . . Walthall, C. L. (2018). Evaluating strategies for sustainable intensification of US agriculture through the long-term agroecosystem research network. *Environmental Research Letters*, *13*(3), 034031.

To, C. K., Chau, K. P., & Kan, C. W. (2020). The logic of innovative value proposition: A schema for characterizing and predicting business model evolution. *Journal of Business Research*, *112*, 502–520.

Tucci, C. L. (2022). The many sides of business model innovation. *Management and Organization Review*, *18*(1), 209–211.

Tucci, C. L., Afuah, A., & Viscusi, G. (Eds.). (2018). *Creating and capturing value through crowdsourcing*. Oxford University Press.

Turoń, K. (2022). From the classic business model to open innovation and data sharing – The concept of an open car-sharing business model. *Journal of Open Innovation: Technology, Market, and Complexity*, *8*(1), 36.

Zott, C., Amit, R., & Massa, L. (2011). The business model: Recent developments and future research. *Journal of Management*, *37*(4), 1019–1042.

6 Measures for Business Model 4.0

Balanced scorecard for Business Model 4.0

In the context of value management, an important management concept and instrument is the balanced scorecard (BSC), the principles of which are widely used both in business organizations par excellence and in other institutions of public life (e.g., hospitals, municipalities and universities). Shaping the value of an enterprise is highly dependent on the architecture and elements of business processes. Business processes, by their very nature, generate value for the customer. The value obtained finds expression in profitable sales, customer satisfaction and customer loyalty (Kaplan, 2009, 2011).

The use of the BSC methodology for corporate competitive strategy makes it possible to transform measurement into a management process. The BSC should evolve from sets of measures to a complex system that monitors all services and solutions used at all levels of management and in all organizational units (Nørreklit & Mitchell, 2007; Nair, 2004).

A study conducted by Kaplan and Norton (2001) indicate that the BSC is not only a system for measuring operational performance but is also a strategic management system, which is related to its use in the following key management processes:

- refining the vision and strategy;
- clarifying strategic goals and metrics and integrating them into management systems;
- planning, goal setting and strategic initiatives;
- improving the organization's monitoring, strategy implementation and learning systems.

The development of a BSC mobilizes the company's management to precisely formulate the strategy and vision by detailing the strategic objectives and identifying the key factors influencing their implementation (Rangkuti, 2013). The process of strategy formulation, due to its complexity, requires teamwork among top managers who, despite the different goals they are aiming at as managers, subordinate organizational units, are able to develop a consensus in the

DOI: 10.4324/9781003317401-7

form of a coherent strategy covering the entire organization with its organizational culture and experience (Nørreklit, 2003).

The formulated strategic objectives are forward-looking and must be taken into account in the developed plans. The BSC integrates and enables coordination of the company's ongoing plans, giving the opportunity to define consistent initiatives leading to continuous improvement, process reconstruction or setting restructuring programs. Thus, the charter makes it clear that process reengineering is not just a method aimed at reducing costs but first and foremost at improving and redesigning the processes implemented in the organization (Karathanos & Karathanos, 2005).

The last of the management processes in which the BSC plays an important role is the process of organizational learning at the highest levels of management. The charter serves both to monitor the implementation of the strategy and to take appropriate corrective actions and, if necessary, to design changes to the strategy itself. Implementation of these activities is possible thanks to the feedback on the implementation of the adopted strategy and the assumptions formulated in the charter, which is received and used by management (Chytas et al., 2011). The flow of information generated by the charter influences the process of organizational learning, as it provides managers with information not only about the implementation of the strategy as planned (single-loop learning) but more importantly information about whether the adopted strategy will ensure survival and success (double-loop learning). The result of the double-loop learning process can become an adjustment of the strategy or a complete change of the strategy corresponding to the new market conditions and internal capabilities of the enterprise (Pandey, 2005). The basis of successful strategy implementation becomes the process of information gathering, the process of hypothesis testing, the process of analysis, the process of strategic learning and the process of adaptation (Niven, 2003).

The BSC makes it possible to translate the vision into operational activities and individual goals that can be understood by employees at all levels of the organization. The BSC allows to give a common direction to the activities of all business units and makes all employees do what is optimal for the company. The charter identifies four perspectives: financial, customer, internal processes and development. All perspectives are very important for the company's current and future market success and competitiveness. The financial perspective measures current financial success, the customer perspective identifies the sources of success, which can be market position and customer satisfaction. To achieve financial and market success, an enterprise must have the right business processes, the effectiveness of which is measured from the perspective of internal processes. The market success of a company also depends on its ability to change, the level of flexibility of its processes and further growth (Modell, 2012).

Traditional systems for measuring the effectiveness of strategy implementation are not suited to the environment in which companies operate, for two reasons. First, they deal mainly with historical activities rather than the goals the company wants to achieve in the future (Kaplan & Norton, 1996). Second, they focus strongly on financial indicators, which reflect well the efficiency of managing physical resources, which in developed economies account for a small percentage of the market value of companies. The BSC solves the first problem, as it identifies the factors on which an organization's future financial performance depends and focuses managers' attention and the organization's resources on them. The scorecard also offsets the second problem, as it allows you to effectively manage the transformation of intangible assets into measurable financial results by explaining how intangible assets allow companies to implement the adopted strategy (Stewart & Carpenter-Hubin, 2001).

The BSC makes it possible to measure value for current and future customers. Without detracting from the importance of financial indicators, the charter reveals the factors that shape competitive advantage. The BSC connects the company's strategies with the operational level of management and, while acting as a feedback loop, makes it possible to evaluate the implementation of the strategy on the basis of information on the status of the implementation of processes (Hansen & Schaltegger, 2016).

In general, the BSC is (Lesáková et al., 2016):

- a system for measuring a company's achievements in the spheres of finance, customers, internal processes and development;
- a system for monitoring value creation;
- a system of business management that allows monitoring the degree of implementation of the strategy, taking corrective actions, implementation of the strategic plan in accordance with the assumptions and continuous improvement and optimization of the strategy;
- a coherent and systematized methodology for describing strategy, allowing to translate vision and strategy into measurable specific goals.

The BSC can influence (Chytas et al., 2011):

- increased productivity and efficiency – by focusing on strategic projects and business areas;
- improved utilization of investments in intellectual capital – through motivated employees;
- increase in profits – through the discovery and use of intra-company synergistic potentials in individual areas of the company;
- empowerment of the company and its individual departments – by identifying employees with the company's global strategy and correlating their actions with the overall direction adopted by the company;
- reducing costs – through focusing on a narrow information system.

The implementation of a BSC is particularly beneficial when an enterprise operates in rapidly changing markets. For the introduction of the BSC, it is necessary to identify a set of methods and techniques based on acceptable management principles that will be used to plan, evaluate and control the various stages of the ongoing project related to the development and implementation of the BSC, taking into account the time, budget and requirements. This project requires the identification of the following parameters: scope, quality, cost, time and resources. These parameters are in mutual interdependence, which means that a change in one of them is associated with a change in the others. Taking this aspect into account is a prerequisite for maintaining balance in the project (Nair, 2004).

The development of a BSC model begins with the creation of a corporate scorecard for the entire organization, which at a later stage, can be expanded into the following (Badaway et al., 2016):

1 Functional scorecard – this is a charter for individual functional areas of the organization.
2 Operational scorecard – this is a scorecard for operational areas operating within individual functions.
3 Individual scorecard – this is a card for individual employees.

Management concepts oriented toward increased efficiency and innovation are expected to lead to a consequent increase in the value of the company. In the context of value management, an important management concept and instrument is the BSC. Shaping the value of a Business Model 4.0 is highly dependent on its architecture and business process elements. Business processes, by their very nature, generate value for the customer. The value obtained finds expression in profitable sales, customer satisfaction and customer loyalty, which translates into building a competitive advantage for the company.

The construction of the BSC template for Business Model 4.0 began with the definition of its perspectives. Each perspective was assigned goals, for which measures were defined. Two BSC templates were developed.

Template I – is used to quantitatively measure the value of Business Model 4.0. Template I consists of financial, customer, process and social architecture perspectives. The perspectives along with the objectives and their measures are shown in Table 6.1.

Template II is used to assess the efficiency and competitiveness of business processes as well as the entire Business Model 4.0 in terms of the enterprise's transformation to a smart enterprise. Template II consists of organizational perspective, business processes, technical architecture and knowledge and learning. The perspectives along with the objectives and their measures are shown in Table 6.2.

Objectives were defined for each perspective of the BSC. In terms of the organizational perspective, the following goals have been defined:

- Collaboration and projects – collaboration between people, teams and partners inside and outside the company defined by how projects are managed, how interdisciplinary teams are formed and how partners work

Table 6.1 BSC template I to quantitatively measure the value of Business Model 4.0

Financial perspective	
Goal	Measure
Economic profit (EVA)	€
Return on sales of personalized products	Net profit/sales (%)
Return on sales of personalized services	Net profit/sales (%)
Return on sales of complementary services (servitization)	Net profit/sales (%)
Return on assets	Net profit/assets (%)
Dynamics of net profit	Prior period = 100
Process perspective	
Goal	Measure
New product offerings	Number
New service offerings	Number
Quality of products	% of complaints accepted
Quality of services	% of complaints accepted
Quality of complementary services offered through servitization	% of complaints accepted
New processes	Number
Orders carried out within the network of cooperating companies	Number
Customer perspective	
Goal	Measure
Customer satisfaction	% of customers
Customer loyalty	Number of regular customers
Strategic customer value	Sales/(number of strategic customers)
Sales dynamics	Previous year = 100
Social architecture perspective	
Goal	Measure
Employee innovation	Number of improvements
Productivity of employees	Value of sales per employee
Employee qualifications	Number of employees with higher education
Employee satisfaction	% of satisfied employees

Source: Authors' elaboration.

together to achieve a common vision and goal. Project goals are defined by common performance indicators. Teams can be formed in a flexible and agile manner to solve problems as they arise. Risks, responsibilities and rewards are shared. Teams build a shared knowledge base to enable lessons learned for all teams in the future for continuous improvement.

- Strategy – it includes setting priorities, developing a system of rules, practices and processes for transforming vision into business value. A long-term strategy and an appropriately adapted Smart enterprise management model should be implemented in all areas of the company's operations and remain constantly evolving, taking into account changes in the latest trends in technology, business philosophy and practices.

Table 6.2 BSC template II to assess the effectiveness and competitiveness of the Business Model 4.0 in terms of the transformation of the enterprise to a smart enterprise

Organizational perspective		
Goal	Measure	The size of the measure during the measurement period
Cooperation and projects	Implemented projects	Number
Strategy	Evaluation of the degree of strategy implementation	Scale of 1–5
Employees	Qualitative evaluation of employees	Scale of 1–5
Leadership	Qualitative assessment of leadership	Scale of 1–5
Networking	Implementation of projects within cyber-physical networks	Number of projects implemented
Business process perspective		
Goal	Measure	The size of the measure during the measurement period
Internal process integration	Degree of integration of processes within the enterprise	%
Process integration with the environment	Degree of integration of processes with the environment	%
Process integration in the product life cycle	Degree of integration of processes in the area of product life cycle	%
Integration of processes in the service life cycle	Degree of process integration in the service life cycle area	%
Standardization of technology procurement	Degree of standardization of technology purchases	%
Standardization and optimization of energy efficiency	Degree of standardization and optimization of energy efficiency	%
Cooperation with the customer	The scope of cooperation with the customer	%
Product personalization	Scope of personalization of products	%
	Personalized products, their number in the offer of the company	Number
Service personalization	Scope of personalization of service	%
	Personalized services, their number in the offer of the enterprise	Number

Technical architecture process perspective		
Goal	Measure	The size of the measure during the measurement period
Automation	Degree of automation of processes	%
Connectivity	The amount of data exchange between equipment, machines and computer systems	Quantity of data
Smart technologies	Number of smart technologies	Quantity
Smart product	Number of smart products	Quantity
Smart service	Number of smart services	Quantity
Knowledge and learning perspective		
Goal	Measure	The size of the measure during the measurement period
Employee satisfaction	Percentage of satisfied employees according to surveys	%
	Percentage of employees who have faculty training, licenses, authorizations	%
	Number of employees covered by talent management program	Number
Staff qualifications	Training costs per employee	€
Talent	Number of innovative solutions reported.	Number

Source: Authors' elaboration.

- Employee training, employee competency development, talent management – it is a system of processes and programs that aims to develop the skills, knowledge and competencies of employees to achieve organizational excellence in line with the Industry 4.0 concept.
- Leadership – leadership competence refers to the willingness of the board of directors to harness the potential of the latest trends and technologies to keep the company competitive and efficient. Management should have a well-established knowledge of the latest solutions, be able to implement them on its own within key business areas, while in complementary areas it should use an integrated network with external partners. Management should have an established knowledge of the latest concepts, trends and technologies. This knowledge allows them to implement new solutions to improve more than one area of the business and develop their own initiatives in the future.
- Networking – the enterprise is capable of building cyber-physical networks, sharing knowledge, competencies, spare capacity but also risks with network partners during joint production and/or service projects.

In terms of the business process perspective, the following goals have been defined:

- Internal integration – vertical integration of processes within the company. All data will be comprehensively integrated with related digital tools and systems, and their real-time analysis will allow systems to make autonomous decisions. In-house processes and connected IT systems will be comprehensively integrated and automated. Systems (OT and IT) will be able to actively analyze data in real time and make autonomous decisions based on this to optimize their integrated processes.
- Integration with the environment – horizontal integration of processes across the organization and with stakeholders across the value chain. Data will be comprehensively integrated with related digital tools and systems, and their real-time analysis will allow systems to make autonomous decisions. Supply chain processes and connected digital systems will be comprehensively integrated and automated. The systems will be capable of proactively analyzing data in real time and making autonomous decisions based on this to optimize their integrated processes.
- Product lifecycle integration – the integrated product lifecycle will be the integration of people, processes and systems throughout the product lifecycle, covering the stages of design and development, engineering, manufacturing, customer service, service and sales. The processes that manage the entire product lifecycle and the IT systems connected to them will be comprehensively integrated and automated. The systems will be capable of proactively analyzing data in real time and making autonomous decisions based on this to optimize their integrated processes.

- Standardization of technology purchases – total cost of ownership (TCO) over the life cycle of the investment will be a key bidding criterion for companies. Machines and technologies will be selected in tenders where the key aspect will be the TCO over the planned life cycle of the technology. Purchasing specifications will include requirements for open communication interfaces to the machines, allowing real-time data reading along with a naming structure for variables and attributes. The machine will become part of the Industrial Internet of Things infrastructure immediately after installation at the plant.
- Standardization and optimization of energy efficiency – the enterprise will use machine learning algorithms to support energy cost optimization and recommend changes. The enterprise will establish an interdisciplinary team responsible for energy efficiency.
- Cooperation with the customer – in the Business Model 4.0, cooperation with the customer takes on the dimension of partnership and requires deep communication, interaction and personalization of communication. In cooperation with the company, the customer has the opportunity to individualize the product and co-create it from the very beginning of its creation, that is, from the research and development stage. Co-creation and communication will be possible through the use of digital tools and channels. Communication with customers will take place through online and offline channels and will be personalized and automated.
- Product personalization – will be done through online configurators, the customer will be involved in the co-creation of the product by providing information and guidance necessary for its development, as well as the design of new products. The customer will have the opportunity to individualize and personalize products by using an online tool to configure the parameters of the ordered product. Digital technological solutions and the adopted business strategy will enable the customer to be involved in the co-creation of the product through dialogue, actively providing guidance for its development and the design of new products and testing prototypes.

In terms of the technological perspective, the following goals have been defined:

- Process automation – in the field of production along with internal logistics will be characterized by the implementation of technologies to monitor, control and automate production processes. Processes will be fully automated, flexible, requiring no employee intervention. This will enable collaboration and dynamic interactions within highly autonomous networks (between departments and between partners). Automation in business administration and management will be characterized by the implementation of technology to monitor and control and automate business administrative processes, such as product sales, demand planning, marketing, order fulfillment, human resource (HR) planning and management. Automation within the building infrastructure will be characterized by the implementation of technology to monitor, control and automate processes inside buildings and rooms where production takes place, such as management of HVAC (heat, ventilation and air-conditioning), chillers, refrigeration, security and lighting systems.

- Connectivity in the area of production execution and internal logistics will be characterized by connectivity, the ability to communicate and freely exchange data between equipment, machines and computer systems. Systems and equipment will be secured, capable of real-time interaction and quick and easy reconfiguration. Information exchange and interactions within the network will be done in real time while maintaining data security. There will be the ability to quickly and easily reconfigure the network to accommodate any modifications, enabling scalability. Connectivity for the administration and management of the company will be characterized by the interconnection of devices, machines and computer systems, enabling communication and seamless exchange of data.
- Intelligent technologies – will be used to process and analyze data to optimize existing production processes (both in the OT and IT layers) and to create new intelligent systems and solutions for production and internal logistics. The IT systems used will be capable of predicting and diagnosing potential deviations and making autonomous and intelligent decisions to optimize productivity and resource efficiency. Production equipment, facilities and systems will be able to predict deviations from predetermined parameters and related future states of assets and systems and will be able to diagnose their causes. Systems will make autonomous decisions to optimize productivity and resource efficiency.
- Smart product – the vision of a smart product in the Business Model 4.0 is characterized by the ability to make autonomous, intelligent decisions based on real-time data from sensors embedded in the product. It will also have its digital counterpart, the so-called digital twin, enabling simulation of processes using the product. The data will be comprehensively integrated with related digital tools and their real-time analysis will allow autonomous decisions to be made by systems embedded in the product.

In terms of the knowledge and learning perspective, the following objectives have been defined:

- Employee satisfaction – job satisfaction is a priority of the social architecture area of the Business Model 4.0, which seeks to provide employees with a work–life balance (work–life balance). It is an indispensable part of a company's achievement of high operational efficiency.
- Personnel qualification – the number of employees with specialized education including engineering/technical education. The level of personnel qualification reflects the level of knowledge of the company, affects its

competitiveness and attractiveness from the point of view of customers and business partners.

- Talent – talent management will be a set of activities aimed at seeking, recruiting, developing, valuing and empowering individuals with above-average intellectual skills, as well as on the effective use of these abilities by the company for the implementation of its strategy.
- Employee competence management – a training system aimed at, improving the skills of employees, the enterprise will provide its company with an expert cadre of well-trained employees and thus will increase the efficiency and productivity of their work and the profits of its company. Training will make the staff increase their ingenuity, innovativeness, gaining new insights into the tasks they have been performing routinely so far.
- Employee innovation – indicates the creativity of employees. It will allow the enterprise to achieve success in the market, as well as strive for progress by stimulating and supporting creative and active employees. Innovativeness improves the qualities and competitive abilities of the enterprise due to the need to constantly observe the actions of competitors and the reactions of customers, as well as the need to permanently implement novelties.

The BSC described earlier was implemented at the company, which is a manufacturer of packaging for the meat industry that for years has remained among the leading producers of sausage nets in the Polish and foreign markets. It has been operating in Poland since 1989. Its operations have been fully based on Polish capital from the beginning. The company supplies its products to more than 1,300 meat plants and wholesalers in the country. Abroad, the products are available through a network of more than a thousand distributors in 45 countries throughout Europe, Asia, North and South America and Australia. The company employs nearly 200 people at its production plant and subsidiaries. The business model is based on short lead times, high-quality products, a wide assortment and expert advice. The implementation of the Business Model 4.0 required the company to automate the production process and implement selected tools that make up the production digitalization process based on the Industrial Internet of Things, Big Data and augmented reality. Salespeople are being trained to be very familiar with product characteristics, inspection methods and knowledge of the manufacturing process. Improved business processes use and develop many elements of the social and technical architecture of the business model. The transformation of the business model of the company under study was associated with a significant increase in customer value, the company's financial capital increased, and the nature of competitive advantage changed. The used "template II" of the BSC for assessing the effectiveness and competitiveness of the Business Model 4.0 in terms of the transformation of the enterprise to a smart enterprise is shown in Table 6.3.

Analyzing the data contained in the customer's perspective, it can be seen that Company 1 has kept its assessment of the degree of strategy implementation at a constant "3" in the 2017–2019 surveyed years. There was an increase

Table 6.3 BSC for a food company

Organizational perspective					
Goal	Measure	The size of the measure during the measurement period	Year 1	Year 2	Year 3
Strategy	Evaluation of the degree of implementation of the strategy	Scale of 1–5	3	3	3
Employees	Qualitative evaluation of employees	Scale 1–5	3	3	4
Leadership	Qualitative assessment of leadership	Scale 1–5	3	3	4
Networking	Implementation of projects within cyber-physical networks	Number of projects implemented	0	5	12
Business process perspective					
Goal	Measure	The size of the measure during the measurement period	Year 1	Year 2	Year 3
Internal process integration	Degree of integration of processes within the enterprise	%	45%	60%	65%
Integration of processes with the environment	Degree of integration of processes with the environment	%	5%	15%	15%
Integration of processes in the product life cycle	Degree of integration of processes in the product life cycle area	%	45%	60%	60%
Standardization and optimization of energy efficiency	Degree of standardization and optimization of energy efficiency	%	42%	43%	44%
Cooperation with the customer	The extent of cooperation with the customer	%	46%	50%	52%
Technical architecture process perspective					
Goal	Measure	The size of the measure during the measurement period	Year 1	Year 2	Year 3
Automation	Degree of automation of processes	%	25%	45%	45%
Connectivity	The amount of data exchange between equipment, machines and computer systems	Number of data	10 T	12 T	13 T
Intelligent technologies	Number of smart technologies	Number	6	7	7

Knowledge and learning perspective

Goal	Measure	The size of the measure during the measurement period	Year 1	Year 2	Year 3
Staff qualifications	Percentage of employees with directional education, licenses, authorizations	%	69%	69%	71%
Talents	Number of employees covered by talent management program	Number	6	7	5
Management of staff competencies	Training costs per employee	€	120€	120€	150€
Innovation of employees	Number of innovative solutions reported	Number	21	19	20

Source: Authors' elaboration.

in the qualitative assessment of employees and leadership over the three years studied. In 2018, the first projects within the cyber-physical cooperation network were implemented, and in the following year the number of projects was increased from 5 to 12.

Within the business process perspective, an increase in evaluation parameters was noted in all processes. Process integration with the environment and process integration in the process life cycle in 2018–2019 reached the same value.

In the technical architecture process perspective, the degree of automation was increased from 25% to 45%. There was a continuous increase in the number of data transferred between devices and the number of smart technologies increased – to 7.

In the perspective of knowledge acquisition and learning, staff qualifications increased, with a total of eighteen employees being included in the talent management program. The budget allocated to staff training was increased. Staff innovation as expressed by the number of submitted innovation solutions remained at an average of 20 submissions per year.

Key performance indicators (KPIs)

Key Performance Indicators (KPI) is one of the tools that help manage almost every area of a company. Under this three-letter acronym are various types of metrics with which you can evaluate the functioning of the company, catch areas of inefficiency, track changes over time, assess the effectiveness of employees and so on (Weber & Thomas, 2005; Marr, 2015).

Efficiency can be considered according to different benchmarks, depending on the needs and specifics of a company's operations. In opposition to traditional approaches to measuring efficiency based on financial performance, it is widely accepted that efficiency should be measured using both financial and nonfinancial, quantitative and qualitative indicators. Certainly, an important benchmark for performance measurement is the set goals and objectives (Lindberg et al., 2015). Due to their diversity, it is problematic to adopt a uniform methodology for measuring performance, and therefore each company should individually formulate criteria for performance measurement, appropriately select the yardsticks and tools with which this measurement will be carried out.

The use of KPIs gives you the knowledge to monitor the degree to which managerial objectives are being met in real time – which in turn allows you to make quick decisions, prioritize activities and improve your strategy. These indicators allow you to reduce complex information about the company and its performance to a small number of key data, giving you understandable results from which you can draw conclusions and modify your course of action (Al Dakheel et al., 2020; Badaway et al., 2016).

In the words of Peter Drucker (2014, p. 15), if something can be measured, it can also be managed. However, KPIs do not mean all measurement of information. What is meant here are key indicators – those whose measurement yields meaningful results that reflect the state the company is in and the degree to which its plans are being implemented (Ishaq Bhatti et al., 2014).

It is important, therefore, to select indicators appropriately, since not everything that can be measured is equally important for expanding knowledge and drawing correct conclusions. From the whole range of possibilities available, one should select a few or a dozen indicators that best demonstrate the level of achievement of strategic goals (Chan & Chan, 2004; Parmenter, 2015).

KPIs set by different companies or organizations will vary due to conditions such as the industry, size of the company or its specific characteristics. To achieve meaningful results, it is necessary to properly define the indicator in relation to the company and its specific needs and to set targets to be achieved (Sanchez & Robert, 2010). The indicator must address the information that is key and assume an achievable goal. It is also necessary to define the time period over which the indicator should achieve the desired value (Souifi et al., 2022). Measuring performance using KPIs is intended to increase knowledge and improve company performance. KPIs help managers define and achieve operational and strategic goals.

The use of KPIs gives managers the knowledge to monitor the degree to which objectives are being met on an ongoing basis – and this, in turn, makes it possible to make quick decisions, prioritize activities and improve the company's development strategy (Lamban et al., 2022; Dominquez et al., 2019).

A useful set of KPIs in an entity should meet the following conditions (Grycuk, 2010):

- the indicators should address issues that are important to the unit, that is, those that are identified in its strategy or directly serve its implementation;
- the indicators are adapted to the situation and the specifics of the sector in which the entity operates;
- the number of indicators should not be too large, as measurement should focus on monitoring key processes rather than measuring everything;
- each indicator must have a specific benchmark (standard) for a given period of study, for example, these are the results achieved by the entity in previous periods;
- the benchmarks should be adjusted (raised) in subsequent periods to stimulate continuous improvement;
- only those indicators should be selected whose results are really influenced by employees;
- most indicators should focus on the processes of satisfying customer needs and measuring customer satisfaction;
- the costs of data collection should not be higher than the benefits of using indicators.

Table 6.4 defines KPIs for the Business Model 4.0 in the area of success factors and in the area of technical architecture. Each key success indicator is a target

Table 6.4 KPIs for Business Model 4.0

KPIs/Goal	*Measure*	*Source of information*	*Measurement frequency*
Critical success factors			
Shift management	Number of changes initiated	All company departments	Once per month
	Number of implemented changes	All company departments	Every 3 months
Competency	Number of training sessions	HR department Training department	Every 6 months
Cooperation within network	Number of networks established for implementation of specific task/project/product	Procurement department, logistics, production, sales, service	Once per month
	Number of orders carried out in network	Procurement department, logistics, production, sales, service	Once per month
Automation and robotization of production system			
Autonomous robots	Number of autonomous robots	Production department, logistics	Every 6 months
Simulations			
Computer programs for product modeling	Number of programs	IT department Production department	Every 6 months
Process simulation programs	Number of programs	IT department Production department	Every 6 months
Software integration			
Data freely transferred between systems	Amount of data sent	IT department	Once per month
	Number of systems between which data is transferred	IT department	Once per month
Programs/systems used to communicate with supplier	Number of programs/systems	IT department	Once per month
Use of electronic Kanban cards	Number of electronic Kanban Cards used	Production department	Once per month
Programs/systems/tools used to communicate with client	Number of programs/systems/tools used to communicate with client	IT department Production department Sales department Logistics department Marketing department	Every 6 months

Industrial Internet of Things, Internet of Services			
Application of sensors collecting information	Number of sensors installed	Production department	Once per month
	Number of product types with sensors	Production department	Once per month
	Number of production cells where sensors are mounted	Production department	Once per month
Cybersecurity			
Data security level	Number of cyberattacks	IT department	Once per month
	Number and frequency of backups performed	IT department	Once per month
Cloud			
Cloud-based software	Number of cloud-based applications	IT department	Once per month
	Amount of data stored in cloud	IT department	Once per month
Use of incremental technologies			
Product prototypes	Number of prototypes of new products made	Design department (It can be organizational unit in production department)	Once per month
Manufacture of products	Number of manufactured products	Production department	Once per month
Augmented reality (e.g., glasses displaying instructions superimposed on observed object)			
Operator support	Number of production stations equipped with glasses	Production department	Every 3 months
Searching for materials in warehouse	Number of production stations equipped with glasses	Production department Warehouse	Every 3 months
Equipment repair	Number of devices equipped with glasses	Production department	Every 3 months
	Number of failures removed using glasses	Service department	Once per month
Virtual training	Number of training sessions conducted in virtual format	HR department	Once per month
	Number of employees trained	HR department	Once per month
Large data sets			
Data on product quality	Number of products manufactured	Production department	Once per month
	Number of defective products	Production department Quality department	Once per month
Machine data	Number of failures	Production department service	Once per month

(*Continued*)

Table 6.4 (Continued)

KPIs/Goal	*Measure*	*Source of information*	*Measurement frequency*
	Machine downtime due to breakdowns	Production departmentservice	Once per month
	Machine downtime due to need to change it	Production department service	Once per month
	Machine downtime caused by its maintenance	Production department service	Once per month
	Machine downtime due to its use	Production department	Once per month
Use of collected data in real time	Amount of data used and its purpose	All departments	Once per month
Autonomous systems based on AI	Number of such systems	All departments	Every 6 months
Digital process twin that allows for ongoing comparison of process with reference model			
Changes made to process	Number of changes introduced in process	All departments	Every 6 months
	Number of processes changed		
Customization			
Product's pure customization	Number of products offered in each option	Marketing department	Once per month
	Number of products produced in each option	Sales department	
Product's tailored customization			
Product's customized standardization		Production department	
Product's pure standardization			
AI (machine learning)			
Autonomous process implemented by AI	Number of processes	All departments	Every 6 months
Process supported by AI			

Source: Authors' elaboration.

for which a measure is defined, the source of information and the recommended frequency of measurement are indicated.

The set of KPIs of the Business Model 4.0, presented in Table 6.4, is a proposal of goals for managers, who, based on it, should modify it in relation to a particular enterprise, its specifics, structure, business profile and so on. The use of KPIs provides knowledge that allows you to monitor the level of implementation of managerial objectives on an ongoing basis – and this, in turn, allows you to make quick decisions, prioritize activities and improve strategies. These indicators allow you to reduce information about the company to those key ones, giving you understandable results from which you can draw conclusions and modify the way you operate.

It is important to choose the right indicators, because not everything that can be measured in a company is equally important for expanding knowledge about the efficiency of processes and drawing the right conclusions for the business model. From the whole range of available options, one should choose a few indicators that best show the level of achievement of defined strategic goals corresponding to the business model adopted by the enterprise.

Bibliography

Al Dakheel, J., Del Pero, C., Aste, N., & Leonforte, F. (2020). Smart buildings features and key performance indicators: A review. *Sustainable Cities and Society*, *61*, 102328.

Badawy, M., Abd El-Aziz, A., Idress, A., Hefny, H., & Hossam, S. (2016). A survey on exploring key performance indicators. *Future Computing and Informatics Journal*, *1*(1–2), 47–52.

Chan, A., & Chan, A. (2004). Key performance indicators for measuring construction success. *Benchmarking: An International Journal*, *11*, 203–221. https://doi.org/10.1108/14635770410532624

Chytas, P., Glykas, M., & Valiris, G. (2011). A proactive balanced scorecard. *International Journal of Information Management*, *31*(5), 460–468.

Domínguez, E., Pérez, B., Rubio, A., & Zapata, M. (2019). A taxonomy for key performance indicators management. *Computer Standards & Interfaces*, *64*, 24–40.

Drucker, F. (2014). *Zawód menedżer*. Wydawnictwo MT Biznes.

Grycuk, A. (2010). Kluczowe wskaźniki efektywności (KPI) jako narzędzie doskonalenia efektywności operacyjnej firm produkcyjnych zorientowanych na lean. *Przegląd Organizacji*, *2*, 28–31.

Hansen, E., & Schaltegger, S. (2016). The sustainability balanced scorecard: A systematic review of architectures. *Journal Bussines Ethics*, *133*, 193–221.

Ishaq Bhatti, M., Awan, H. M., & Razaq, Z. (2014). The key performance indicators (KPIs) and their impact on overall organizational performance. *Quality & Quantity*, *48*(6), 3127–3143.

Kaplan, R. (2009). Conceptual foundations of the balanced scorecard. *Handbooks of Management Accounting Research*, *3*, 1253–1269.

Kaplan, R. (2011). *Balanced scorecard*. ESENSI.

Kaplan, R., & Norton, D. (1996, January–February). Using the balanced scorecard as a strategic management system. *Harvard Business Review*.

Kaplan, R., & Norton, D. (2001). *The balanced scorecard*. PWN.

Karathanos, D., & Karathanos, P. (2005). Applying the balanced scorecard to education. *Journal of Education for Business, 80*(4), 222–230.

Lambán, M., Morella, P., Royo, J., & Sánchez, J. (2022). Using industry 4.0 to face the challenges of predictive maintenance: A key performance indicators development in a cyber physical system. *Computers & Industrial Engineering, 171*, 108400. https://doi.org/10.1016/j.cie.2022.108400

Lesáková, Ľ., & Dubcová, K. (2016). Knowledge and use of the balanced scorecard method in the businesses in the Slovak republic. *Procedia, Social and Behavioral Sciences, 230*, 39–48.

Lindberg, C., Tan, S., Yan, J., & Starfelt, F. (2015). Key performance indicators improve industrial performance. *Energy Procedia, 75*, 1785–1790.

Marr, B. (2015). *Key performance indicators for dummies*. John Wiley & Sons.

Modell, S. (2012). The politics of the balanced scorecard. *Journal of Accounting & Organizational Change, 8*, 475–489. https://doi.org/10.1108/18325911211273482

Nair, M. (2004). *Essentials of balanced scorecard*. John Wiley & Sons.

Niven, P. (2003). *Balanced scorecard. Step by step for government and nonprofit agencies*. Wiley.

Nørreklit, H. (2003). The balanced scorecard: What is the score? A theoretical analysis of the balanced scorecard. *Accounting, Organizations and Society, 28*(6), 591–619.

Nørreklit, H., & Mitchell, F. (2007). The balanced scorecard. *Issues in Management Accounting, 3*, 175–198.

Pandey, I. M. (2005). Balanced scorecard: Myth and reality. *Vikalpa, 30*(1), 51–66.

Parmenter, D. (2015). *Key performance indicators: Developing, implementing, and using winning KPIs*. John Wiley & Sons.

Rangkuti, F. (2013). *SWOT – Balanced scorecard*. Gramedia Pustaka Utama.

Sanchez, H., & Robert, B. (2010). Measuring portfolio strategic performance using key performance indicators. *Project Management Journal, 41*(5), 64–73.

Souifi, A., Boulanger, Z., Zolghadri, M., Barkallah, M., & Haddar, M. (2022). Uncertainty of key performance indicators for Industry 4.0: A methodology based on the theory of belief functions. *Computers in Industry, 140*, 103666. https://doi.org/10.1016/j.compind.2022.103666

Stewart, A. C., & Carpenter-Hubin, J. (2001). The balanced scorecard. *Planning for Higher Education*, 37–42.

Weber, A., & Thomas, R. (2005). *Key performance indicators. Measuring and managing the maintenance function*. Ivara Corporation.

Conclusion

The Fourth Industrial Revolution has introduced significant changes in the functioning of modern enterprises which implies the need to develop new innovative customer-oriented value creation strategies. Modern enterprises are forced to implement new digital technologies and reorganize their network-oriented business processes. The SME sector in particular expects ready-made models for operating in a dynamically changing market and business models to reduce the risks associated with permanent change. Hence the need to develop Business Model 4.0, aimed at offering unique added value to the customer in the most cost-effective way possible for the company. A Business Model 4.0 dedicated to the SME sector should encourage cooperation among all participants in the value chain, including motivating customer loyalty to the supplier (manufacturer).

The idea of creating a Business Model 4.0 supported by e-business platforms is particularly beneficial for small- and medium-sized enterprises. The idea of clustering enterprises around a platform can be an excellent introduction to the process of adapting the potential of enterprises to the concept of Industry 4.0 and 5.0. It can point them to the directions of development of know-how, identify the necessary resources, competencies to be developed and used in the future in building new networks oriented to personalized production.

The operation of enterprises within the framework of the proposed business model will certainly increase the productivity of their production resources used within cyber-physical networks. Through such cooperation, the organization operates on the basis of an open business model; that is, the cooperation of various entities to develop the most innovative solutions. This model implies a high degree of openness and transparency on the part of the organization, which chooses to share its resources and encourage other companies (including competitors) to collaborate.

The networking of the economy and the use of modern information and communication technologies are forcing entrepreneurs to change the way they manage a modern enterprise. It is necessary to focus on cooperation, exchange of know-how and resources to meet the requirements of the modern customer. Individualization and the required rapid response in the market means the need to combine the potential of different companies. Hence, it is necessary to invest

DOI: 10.4324/9781003317401-8

in new technologies that enable the use of intelligent, self-communicating and self-steering machines and equipment, which lead to the development of new business models. Observing the global market and the success of business models created by, for example, Uber, Adidas, Google, Allegro/eBay and so on, it can be assumed that the architecture of Business Model 4.0 must be very flexible and oriented toward value creation throughout. Enterprises will therefore have to reorganize their business models on an ongoing basis and change their existing modus operandi to a networked resource service-oriented one. The technical architecture of these models will rapidly absorb the latest technological solutions, supporting the ability to personalize production while keeping prices competitive with mass-produced products. In addition, the social architecture of the models will be based on an organizational culture of agile teams based on virtual collaboration. These teams will be formed on a project-by-project (order-by-order) basis and will span the entire enterprise value chain. This will require the implementation of many changes. Implementation and maintenance of new technologies related to Industry 4.0 will require interdisciplinary knowledge and a combination of technical, organizational and social competencies and skills. The education of future industry employees should also increasingly emphasize the combination of engineering and managerial competencies needed for collaboration, communication and interpersonal relationship-building skills.

The considerations presented in the book are particularly dedicated to executives of small- and medium-sized enterprises who are facing the changes determined by the Fourth Industrial Revolution. It helps understand the challenges and allay doubts and fears related to the absorption of new strategies and business models based on digital technologies.

Index

Note: Page numbers in *italics* indicate a figure and page numbers in **bold** indicate a table on the corresponding page.